HOW TO BE A YOGI

HOW TO BE A YOGI

SWAMI ABHEDANANDA

Published by

FacsiMile Publisher
12 Pragati Market
Ashok Vihar, Ph-2
Delhi - 110052, India
Phone: 011-47034999
Email: www.facsimilepublishers.com
info@facsimilepublishers.com

Distribution Network
gyanbooks.com
India, USA, Canada, UK, Australia

ISBN: 978-93-7106-237-4 (PB)
First Published, 1902

2nd Impression 2025

Printed at: Gyan Press, Delhi.

HOW TO BE A YOGI
Author: SWAMI ABHEDANANDA

How to be a Yogi

Vedânta Philosophy

How to be a Yogi

By

Swâmi Abhedânanda

Published by
The Vedânta Society
New York

Preface

THE Vedânta Philosophy includes the different branches of the Science of Yoga. Four of these have already been treated at length by the Swâmi Vivekânanda in his works on "Râja Yoga," "Karma Yoga," "Bhakti Yoga," and "Jnâna Yoga"; but there existed no short and consecutive survey of the science as a whole. It is to meet this need that the present volume has been written. In an introductory chapter are set forth the true province of religion and the full significance of the word "spirituality" as it is understood in India. Next follows a comprehensive definition of the term "Yoga," with short chapters on each of the five paths to which it is applied, and their respective practices. An exhaustive exposition of the Science of Breathing and its bearing on the highest spiritual development shows the fundamental physiological principles on which the whole training of Yoga is based; while a concluding chapter, under the title "Was Christ a Yogi?" makes plain the direct relation existing between the lofty teachings of Vedânta and the religious faiths of the West. An effort has been made, so far as possible, to keep the text free from technical and Sanskrit terms; and the work should therefore prove of equal value to the student of Oriental thought and to the general reader as yet unfamiliar with this, one of the greatest philosophical systems of the world.

THE EDITOR.

Contents

Introductory

Introductory

TRUE religion is extremely practical; it is, indeed, based entirely upon practice, and not upon theory or speculation of any kind, for religion begins only where theory ends. Its object is to mould the character, unfold the divine nature of the soul, and make it possible to live on the spiritual plane, its ideal being the realization of Absolute Truth and the manifestation of Divinity in the actions of the daily life.

Spirituality does not depend upon the reading of Scriptures, or upon learned interpretations of Sacred Books, or upon fine theological discussions, but upon the realization of unchangeable Truth. In India a man is called truly spiritual or religious not because he has written some book, not because he possesses the gift of oratory and can preach eloquent sermons, but because he expresses divine powers through his words and deeds. A thoroughly illiterate man can attain to the highest state of spiritual perfection without going to any school or university, and without reading any Scripture, if he can conquer his animal nature by realizing his true Self and its relation to the universal Spirit; or, in other words, if he can attain to the knowledge of that Truth which dwells within him, and which is the same as the Infinite Source of existence, intelligence, and bliss. He who has mastered all the Scriptures, philosophies, and sciences, may be regarded by society as an intellectual giant; yet he cannot be equal to that unlettered man who, having realized the eternal Truth, has become one with it, who sees God everywhere, and who lives on this earth as an embodiment of Divinity.

The writer had the good fortune to be acquainted with such a divine man in India. His name was Ramakrishna. He never went to any school, neither had he read any of the Scriptures, philosophies, or scientific treatises of the world, yet he had reached perfection by realizing God through the practice of Yoga. Hundreds of men and women came to see him and were spiritually awakened and uplifted by the divine powers which this illiterate man possessed. To-day he is revered and worshipped by thousands all over India as is Jesus the Christ in Christendom. He could expound with extraordinary clearness the subtlest problems of philosophy or of science, and answer the most intricate questions of clever theologians in such a masterly way as to dispel all doubts concerning the matter in hand. How could he do this without reading books? By his wonderful insight into the true nature of things, and by that Yoga power which made him directly perceive things which cannot be revealed by the senses. His spiritual eyes were open; his sight could penetrate through the thick veil of ignorance that hangs before the vision of ordinary mortals, and which prevents them from knowing that which exists beyond the range of sense perception.

These powers begin to manifest in the soul that is awakened to the ultimate Reality of the universe. It is then that the sixth sense of direct perception of higher truths develops and frees it from dependence upon the sense powers. This sixth sense or spiritual eye is latent in each individual, but it opens in a few only among millions, and they are known as Yogis. With the vast majority it is in a rudimentary state, covered by a thick veil. When, however, through the practice of Yoga it unfolds in a man, he becomes conscious of the higher invisible realms and of everything that exists on the soul plane. Whatever he says harmonizes with the sayings and writings of all the great Seers of Truth of every age and clime. He does not study books; he has no need to do so, for he knows all that the human intellect can conceive. He can grasp the purport of a book without reading its text; he also understands how much the human mind can express through words, and he is familiar with that which is beyond thoughts and which consequently can never be expressed by words.

Before arriving at such spiritual illumination he goes through divers stages of mental and spiritual evolution, and in consequence knows all that can be experienced by a human intellect. He does not, however, care to remain confined within the limit of sense perception, and is not contented with the intellectual apprehension of relative reality, but his sole aim is to enter into the realm of the Absolute, which is the beginning and end of phenomenal objects and of relative knowledge. Thus striving for the realization of the highest, he does not fail to collect all relative knowledge pertaining to the world of phenomena that comes in his way, as he marches on toward his destination, the unfoldment of his true Self.

Our true Self is all-knowing by its nature. It is the source of infinite knowledge within us. Being bound by the limitations of time, space, and causation, we cannot express all the powers that we possess in reality. The higher we rise above these limiting conditions, the more we can manifest the divine qualities of omniscience and omnipotence. If, on the contrary, we keep our minds fixed upon phenomena and devote the whole of our energy to acquiring knowledge dependent entirely upon sense perceptions, shall we ever reach the end of phenomenal knowledge, shall we ever be able to know the real nature of the things of this universe? No; because the senses cannot lead us beyond the superficial appearance of sense objects. In order to go deeper in the realm of the invisible we invent instruments, and with their help we are able to penetrate a little further; but these instruments, again, have their limit. After using one kind of instrument, we become dissatisfied with the results and search for some other which may reveal more and more, and thus we struggle on, discovering at each step how poor and helpless are the sense powers in the path of the knowledge of the Absolute. At last we are driven to the conclusion that any instrument, no matter how fine, can never help us to realize that which is beyond the reach of sense-perception, intellect, and thought.

So, even if we could spend the whole of our time and energy in studying phenomena, we shall never arrive at any satisfactory result or be able to see things as they are in reality. The knowledge of to-day, gained by the help of certain instruments, will be the ignorance of tomorrow, if we get better instruments. The knowledge of last year is already the ignorance of the present year; the knowledge of this century will be ignorance in the light of the discoveries of a new century.

The span of one human life is, therefore, too short to even attempt to acquire a correct knowledge of all things existing on the phenomenal plane. The life-time of hundreds of thousands of generations, nay, of all humanity, seems too short, when we consider the infinite variety to be found in the universe, and the countless number of objects that will have to be known before we can reach the end of knowledge. If a man could live a million years, keeping his senses in perfect order during that long period, and could spend every moment in studying nature and in diligently endeavoring to learn every minute detail of phenomenal objects, would his search after knowledge be fulfilled at the expiration of that time? Certainly not; he would want still more time, a finer power of perception, a keener intellect, a subtler understanding; and then he might say, as did

Sir Isaac Newton after a life of tireless research, " I have collected only pebbles on the shore of the ocean of knowledge." If a genius like Newton could not even reach the edge of the water of that ocean, how can we expect to cross the vast expanse from shore to shore in a few brief years? Thousands of generations have passed away, thousands will pass, yet must the knowledge regarding the phenomena of the universe remain imperfect. Veil after veil may be removed, but veil after veil will remain behind. This was understood by the Yogis and Seers of Truth in India, who said: " Innumerable are the branches of knowledge, but short is our time and many are the obstacles in the way; therefore wise men should first struggle to know that which is highest."

Here the question arises: Which is the highest knowledge? This question is as old as history; it has puzzled the minds of the philosophers, scientists, and scholars of all ages and all countries. Some have found an answer to it, others have not. The same question was voiced in ancient times by Socrates, when he went to the Delphic oracle and asked: "Of all knowledge which is the highest?" To which came the answer, "Know thyself."

We read in one of the Upanishads that a great thinker, after studying all the philosophies and sciences known at that time, came to a Seer of Truth and said: "Sir, I am tired of this lower knowledge that can be gained from books or through the study of the world of phenomena; it no longer satisfies me, for science cannot reveal the ultimate Truth; I wish to know that which is the highest. Is there anything by knowing which I can know the reality of the universe?"

The sage replied: "Yes, there is; and that knowledge is the highest, by knowing which you can know the true nature of everything in the universe." And he continued, "Know thyself. If thou canst learn the true nature of thine own self, thou wilt know the reality of the universe. In thy true Self thou wilt find the Eternal Truth, the Infinite Source of all phenomena. By knowing this thou wilt know God and His whole creation." As by knowing the chemical properties of one drop of water, we know the properties of all water wherever it appears, so by knowing who and what we are in reality, we shall realize the final Truth. Man is the epitome of the universe. That which exists in the macrocosm is to be found in the microcosm. Therefore the knowledge of one's true Self is the highest of all knowledge. Our real Self is divine and one with

God. This may seem to us at present a mere theory, but the nearer we approach the ultimate Truth, the more clearly shall we understand that it is not a theory but a fact, that now we are dreaming in the sleep of ignorance and fancying ourselves this or that particular person. But as all experience gained in dreams afterwards appears of little consequence; so, waking up from this sleep, we shall find that the knowledge of phenomenal nature, upon which we place so much value at present, is of little importance. We shall then realize that all research in the various branches of science depends upon Self-knowledge, and that Self-knowledge is the foundation upon which the structure of phenomenal knowledge is built.

Knowledge of the Self or Atman is therefore the highest of all. It is the ideal of the Science of Yoga, and should be the aim of our life. We should hold it as our first duty to acquire this Self-knowledge before we try to know anything concerning the objects of sense-perception. How can we gain it? Not from books, not through the study of external phenomena, but by studying our own nature, and by practicing the different branches of Yoga.

What is Yoga?

What is Yoga?

In all the Sacred Writings of the world as well as in the lives of the inspired teachers, prophets, saints, and Seers of Truth, we find frequent descriptions of miraculous events and powers, which, admitting a certain measure of exaggeration, must still have had some foundation in fact. We, indeed, know that from time immemorial in every age and in every country there have arisen among the different nations persons who could read the thoughts of others, who could foresee and could prophesy that which afterwards came to pass; but most of these people did not understand the causes of their own peculiar gifts, and tried to explain them by attributing them to the influence of external Beings, whom they called by various names—gods, angels, good or evil spirits.

Some among them even fancied that they were especially chosen to be the instruments of these higher powers and sought to be worshipped as the elect of God or of their particular deity, just as the leaders of certain sects in this country today desire to be adored by their followers. In some instances, those who possessed these unusual powers were looked upon as divine exceptions, as Jesus by the Christians, Mahomet by the Mahometans, and Buddha by the Buddhists. Others again were condemned as sorcerers or witches, and the fear aroused by such persecutions led to the secret practice of divers methods which resulted in still further extraordinary manifestations.

These methods were never written down, but were passed orally from the master to the disciple, who in turn carefully guarded them as sacred mysteries. This is the reason why among ancient nations there grew up so many secret societies, the object of which was to develop certain powers through various kinds of discipline and practices. The Egyptians, the Essenes, Gnostics, Manicheans, Neo-Platonists, and the Christian mystics of the middle ages all had their secret organizations, and some of them still exist, as, for example, the Masonic Lodge. None of the members of these societies ever gave out their secret instructions, nor did they write any books offering a logical or scientific explanation of their practices. Therefore, while there were some among them who advanced far in the attainment of higher powers, the unusual manifestations resulting therefrom were never understood by Western nations, neither were they generalized into a system or science.

In ancient India, on the contrary, as there was no fear of persecution, the case was altogether different. Every Hindu was obliged, as a part of his religious duty, to develop through daily practice certain powers and to strive to attain to the realization of higher truths. In the streets, on the market-place, in the courts, and on the battle-field were many who had not only reached such realization, but who had carefully classified their experiences and discovered those laws which govern our higher nature and upon which was gradually built up the profound Science of Yoga.

Thus we see that this science, like all others, was based on experience; while the method used in it was the same as that employed by modern science in making all its discoveries of natural law—the method of observation and experiment. This method is regarded in the West as a distinctly modern innovation, but as a matter of fact it was adopted in India in very ancient times by the "Rishis," or Seers of Truth. Through the process of close observation and constant experiment they discovered the finer forces of nature, as also the laws that govern our physical, mental, and spiritual being. The truths thus gained through their own experience and investigations, they wrote down in books, preached in public, and expounded to their pupils. Before, however, they affirmed anything about the nature of the soul or God, they had realized it. Before they asked a disciple to practice anything they had practiced it themselves, and had obtained definite results from that practice.

In this way, as the outcome of ages of research in the realms of nature, carried on by a succession of earnest seekers after light, there grew up in India various systems of science, philosophy, psychology, metaphysics, and religion, both speculative and practical, which were grouped under the one common name, "Aryan Religion." The term "religion" was used to include all, because at no epoch in India has religion been separated from these different branches or from the general conduct of every-day existence; and the methods by which these scientific truths were applied in the daily life of an individual to further his spiritual development, were called by the general term "Yoga."

"Yoga" is a Sanskrit word commonly used to signify the practical side of religion; and the first concern of the training for which it stands, is to enforce proper obedience to the laws of our moral and physical nature, upon which depend the attainment of perfect health and of moral and spiritual perfection. In Western countries the word has been grossly misunderstood and misused by many writers, who have employed it in the sense of jugglery, hypnotism, trickery, and fraud. Whenever people hear the word "Yogi," which signifies one who practices Yoga, they think of some kind of juggler, or charlatan, or identify him with a fakir or one who practices black magic. The Theosophists have been more or less responsible for this abuse of the term; but those who have studied the Sacred Books of India, as, for instance, the Bhagavad Gita or Song Celestial, as Sir Edwin Arnold calls it in his translation, will remember that each chapter of that Celestial Song is devoted to some kind of "Yoga," or method of realizing the Ultimate Truth and of attaining the highest wisdom; and that a "Yogi" is one who through various practices reaches the highest ideal of religion. This highest ideal, according to the Bhagavad Gita, is the union of the individual soul with the Universal Spirit.

Hindu writers, however, have used the word "Yoga" in various other senses. I will mention a few of them in order to give some conception of the vastness of the field covered by this term. First, "Yoga" means the union of two external objects. Second, the mixing of one thing with another. Third, the interrelation of the causes which produce a common effect. Fourth, the orderly equipment of a soldier or of any person in any profession. Fifth, the application, discrimination, and reasoning that is necessary for the discovery of a certain truth. Sixth, that power of sound which makes it convey a specific idea. Seventh, the preservation of what one possesses. Eighth, the transformation of one thing into another. Ninth, the union of one soul with another or with the universal Spirit. Tenth, the flowing of a thought current towards an object. Eleventh, the restraint of all thought action through concentration and meditation. Thus we see how many different branches of art, science, psychology, philosophy, and religion are included in the various definitions of this one word. It seems, indeed, in its scope and range to take in every department of nature. If, however, we consider the literal meaning of the word, we shall more easily understand why it is so all-inclusive.

It is derived from the Sanskrit root "Yuj," which means to join. The English word "yoke" also comes from the same root. Originally the literal signification of the two words was almost the same. The root-verb "Yuj" signifies to join oneself to something, or to harness oneself for some task. Thus in its primary meaning it conveys the same idea of preparing for hard work as the common English expressions "to go into harness," or "to buckle to." The effort required is mental or physical, according to the object in view. If the object be the acquirement of perfect health or longevity, then the effort of both mind and body to accomplish this through certain practices is called "Yoga." So is it again if the object be the development of psychic powers. The same word is used likewise to indicate the mental training necessary for the attainment of self-control, of the union of the individual soul with God, of divine communion or of spiritual perfection. Volumes upon volumes have been written in India describing the different branches and methods of this applied science of "Yoga," and the various ideals that can be attained through its practice; also what qualifications fit a beginner for undertaking any of these methods, what stages he must pass through in order to reach the goal, what obstacles stand in the way, and how they can be overcome.

Patience and perseverance are absolutely necessary for any one who desires to enter upon the path of Yoga; those who are not patient cannot hope to arrive at true realization. Those, again, who take it up out of curiosity or through an impulse of temporary enthusiasm, must not expect to get results, and must not blame the teacher for their failure to do so, since the fault is entirely their own. The same teachings, when carried out with understanding and in the right spirit, will bring wonderful results. They will only come, however, to the student who follows strictly the instructions of a living master, who will direct him in the practice of both physical and mental exercises.

Aspirants to the study of Yoga can be divided into three classes: First, those who are born Yogis. There are some who, having practiced Yoga in a previous incarnation, come here as awakened souls, and as such manifest remarkable powers from their very childhood. Their natural tendency is to lead a pure life, for right living and right thinking are their sole concern, and they possess wonderful powers of self-control and of concentration. Sense pleasures and those things which fascinate the ordinary mind have no charm for them. Even when they are surrounded by all the comforts of life and have every material resource at their command, they yet feel like strangers in a strange land. Few there are who can understand properly the mental condition of these characters. Physicians may be brought to them, but medical treatment may only make them worse; the writer knows of cases where harm has been done in this way. By the law of attraction, however, they are bound to be drawn sooner or later into the companionship of some Yogi. Here they find exactly what their inner nature has been craving, and at once they feel happy and at home. The instructions of the Yogi appeal to their minds; they begin the practice of Yoga under his direction, and proving easy and natural to them, they soon obtain excellent results. Thus from youth they take up the thread of the practice at the very point where they dropped it in their past existence; and through a firm determination to overcome all obstacles in their way, they progress rapidly and gradually attain to the highest ideal of spiritual life. Nothing in the world can prevent their onward march, so intense and strong is their longing for realization.

The second class includes those who are born as half-awakened souls. In need of further experience, they go through various paths without finding the right one. They take each new step tentatively, and in this constant experimenting, they waste a great deal of energy and a large portion of their lives. If such partially awakened souls, following out a tendency created in their previous existence, have the good fortune to come in contact with a Yogi and take up the practice of Yoga, they may, through perseverance and earnestness, achieve much in this life, although they will necessarily advance more slowly in the path of spirituality than those who belong to the first class.

In the third class are to be found all those unawakened souls who begin their search after Truth and the practice of Yoga for the first time in this life. Even from childhood they are irresistibly drawn towards sense objects and sense pleasures; and if they take up the practice of Yoga, they find great difficulty in following its teachings and meet numerous obstacles along the way. Their environment is not favorable for the practice, and even when they try, they cannot easily conquer it. Their health is not good, their mind is scattered, and they suffer from various kinds of disease and mental disturbance. They also lack determination, find it wellnigh impossible to control the senses, and have to fight hard to adjust their mode of living to the new requirements. With so much to contend against they naturally obtain but small results even after long practice. If, however, such persons can persevere and strengthen their wills through a slow and regular practice of Hatha Yoga, struggling manfully to overcome the many obstacles in their way by the practice of breathing exercises and by following the directions of a competent teacher, who understands them, they may in this life be able to control in a large measure their physical health and acquire a certain amount of Yoga power. Hatha Yoga is especially useful for this class of aspirants. Through the practice of breathing exercises they will gradually gain control over their bodies, and will, in course of time, be prepared for the study of Râja Yoga, which will arouse the powers latent in their souls.

Hatha Yoga

HATHA YOGA is that branch of the Science of Yoga which teaches how to conquer hunger, thirst, and sleep; how to overcome the effects of heat and cold; how to gain perfect health and cure disease without using drugs; how to arrest the untimely decay of the body resulting from the waste of vital energy; how to preserve youth even at the age of one hundred without having a single hair turn grey, and how thus to prolong life in this body for an indefinite period. Anyone who practices it will in the course of time acquire marvellous powers; powers indeed, which must dumbfound a psychologist or anatomist.

A few years ago a Hatha Yogi was brought to England. Although in middle life he looked like a boy of eighteen. Not only was his physical condition perfect, but through practice he had mastered eighty-four postures of the body. He could bend his limbs in so astonishing a way that it seemed as if his joints must be unattached, while his bones were as though made of some elastic substance. Many English physicians and surgeons came to see him and were amazed at the extraordinary positions of his limbs. They brought a skeleton and tried to fix its bones in the same positions, but could not do so without breaking them. Afterwards they reached the conclusion that if the bones were once fixed in those positions the limbs would be unfitted for any kind of work. Yet the example of the Yogi openly contradicted their statements. His limbs were strong and of good use to him in every possible way. He could walk, lift heavy weights, and move about with absolute ease. The writer himself saw him in India, and also other Hatha Yogis who could accomplish equally wonderful feats. The primary object of these various postures described in Hatha Yoga is to gain control over the involuntary muscles of the body, which is impossible to the ordinary man. We all possess this power latent within us, but the Hatha Yogis were the first to discover a scientific method by which it could be developed.

All Hatha Yogis eat very little, but they can also go entirely without food for days and even for months, and succeed in conquering sleep. The author knew of one who had not slept for twelve years, and who was nevertheless in perfect health. He has also seen a Hatha Yogi who usually ate, for instance, a piece of unleavened bread in twenty-four hours, and who refused to wear warm clothing in the coldest winter weather, and yet who voluntarily worked hard as a street laborer without showing the least sign of fatigue. It may seem impossible to the majority of people, who have made themselves such slaves to sleep and food as to imagine that if they do not sleep eight or nine hours out of the twenty-four and eat pounds of flesh, they cannot live. Hatha Yogis are the living contradictions of such opinions. Perhaps the reader is familiar with the account of that Yogi who was buried alive for forty days in an hermetically sealed box, with a guard of English officers to watch the spot night and day. During these forty days the Yogi could neither eat, sleep, nor breathe, yet at their expiration he was brought back to consciousness without any ill effects and he lived for many years.*

* For fuller account see "Law of Psychic Phenomena," by Thomas Jay Hudson, page 313.

Then again these same Yogis who do not eat, sleep, or drink for a long period, can, if they wish, eat as much as ten persons at one time without suffering any unpleasant consequences. Of course they do not eat any kind of meat. They digest their food consciously, as it were. They claim that by a third eye they can, so to speak, see what is going on in their internal organs. Why should this seem incredible to us when the discovery of the Roentgen rays has proved everything to be transparent?

Some of the Hatha Yogis have extraordinary eyesight. They can not only perceive objects at a great distance, but can also see clearly in complete darkness, even being able to pick up a pin from the floor without the least glimmer of ordinary light to guide them. This will not appear so strange when we remember that there is invisible light in the atmosphere of a perfectly dark room. If we can learn to use this atmospheric light, imperceptible to the common eye, and can develop our eyesight, there is no reason why we should not see things in the dark. The Yogis understand this and know the method by which the power of eyesight can be developed. As regards distinguishing objects at a great distance, this is not so difficult to believe since we know that there are persons living, not Yogis, who can see the moons of Jupiter without the help of any instrument.

This branch of optical science in Hatha Yoga is called in Sanskrit "Trâtaka" Yoga. It teaches, among other things, how, through gazing on one object and at the same time performing certain special breathing exercises, many optical maladies can be cured as well as the power of sight strengthened. The authentic records of Hatha Yogis vouch for the fact that it produces many beneficial effects when properly practiced under the direction of a competent master of Hatha Yoga.

A Yogi who is expert in this science of optics can fascinate or madden another by his optical powers. The process of hypnotism or mesmerism verifies this claim. A Yogi can likewise read the thoughts of another by looking at his eyes; for according to the Yogi the eye is the index of the mind. Here it may be asked, how do the Yogis acquire these powers? They do not get them from outside. These powers are dormant in every individual, and through practice the Yogis bring them out. They say: "Whatever exists in the universe (the macrocosm) exists also in the human body (the microcosm)." That is, the finer forces exist potentially in our own organism, and if we study our nature carefully we shall be able to know all the forces and the laws which govern the universe.

Hatha Yoga, again, teaches the cure of disease through breathing exercises and the regulation of diet and of the general habits of the daily life. But it does not claim that physical health is the same as spirituality. On the contrary, it tells us that if a healthy body were a sign of spirituality, then wild animals and savages who enjoy perfect health would be exceedingly spiritual; yet they are not, as we know. The principal idea of these Yogis is that physical maladies are obstacles in the path of spiritual progress, while a healthy body furnishes one of the most favorable conditions for the realization of the highest spiritual truths in this life. Those who do not possess good health should, therefore, begin to practice Hatha Yoga.

In the practice of Hatha Yoga strict dietetic rules must be observed. Anything that is sharp, sour, pungent, or hot, like mustard, liquors, fish, flesh of animals, curd, buttermilk, oil cakes, carrots, onions, and garlic should not be eaten. Food, again, which, having been once cooked, has grown cold and been rewarmed, should be avoided; as should also excess of salt or acidity, or that which is hard to digest. Rice, barley, wheat, milk, sugar, honey, and butter are good for a Hatha Yogi's diet. The manner in which Americans live in hotels and boarding-houses, where the food is often unclean, is far from favorable to this practice. Food cooked for hundreds of people in a restaurant cannot be equally good for all and may easily cause disease. Those who wish to enjoy perfect health must be careful about what they eat; they must also observe all the laws of hygiene regarding cleanliness of the body, fresh air, and pure water. They should not live in over-heated houses; neither should they indulge in artificial stimulants, especially beer, wine, and coffee. The habit of excessive coffee-drinking is a serious menace to the American nation. Many people are already suffering from nervous prostration as a result of indulgence in this direction, and there are very few cases in which the nervous system will not be affected by it to some extent.

He who wishes to practice Hatha Yoga should first of all find a Hatha Yogi teacher, who has perfect control over his physical body; and having found him, he should lead a life in strict accord with his instructions. He should live in a secluded spot and where the changes of weather are neither sudden nor extreme. He should be a rigid vegetarian and abstain from all kinds of drinks that stimulate the system. He should never fill the stomach with a large quantity of food. He should observe the moral laws and practice absolute continence. He should learn to control his senses, keep his body clean, and purify his mind by arousing feelings of kindness and love towards all living creatures.

The beginner in this branch of Yoga should gradually conquer the different postures of the body and limbs. These postures are called in Sanskrit *Âsana.* There are altogether eighty-four of them described in the science of Hatha Yoga. Each of these, when practiced with special breathing exercises, develops certain powers latent in the nerve centers and the different organs of the system. Another object in practicing *Âsana* is to remove the

Tamas element which causes heaviness of the body, and to free the system from the effects of cold, catarrh, phlegm, rheumatism, and many other diseases. Some of the exercises increase the action of the stomach and liver, while others regulate the activities of the other organs. Tremor of the body and restlessness of the limbs, which are such frequent obstacles in the way of gaining control over the mind, may easily be removed by the practice of *Âsana.*

The reader may get an idea of the *Âsana* from the following descriptions:

I. Sit cross-legged on the floor, placing the left foot on the right thigh and the right foot on the left thigh, and keeping the body, neck, and head in a straight line.

II. After sitting in this posture, hold the right great toe with the right hand and the left great toe with the left hand (the hands coming from behind the back and crossing each other).

III. Sit straight on a level place, firmly inserting both insteps between the thighs and the calves of the legs.

IV. Assuming posture No. I, insert the hands between the thighs and the calves, and, planting the palms firmly on the ground, lift the body above the seat.

V. Sitting on the floor, stretch the legs straight in front, hold the great toes with the hands without bending the knees.

VI. Having accomplished this posture, touch the knees with the forehead. This *Âsana* rouses gastric fire, makes the loins lean, and removes many diseases.

VII. Holding the toes as in posture V, keep one arm extended and with the other draw the other toe towards your ear as you would do with the string of a bow.

VIII. Plant hands firmly on the ground,

support the weight of the body upon the elbows, pressing them against the sides of the loins. Then raise the feet above the ground, keeping them stiff and straight on a level with the head.

This *Âsana,* according to Hatha Yoga, cures diseases of the stomach, spleen, and liver, and all disorders caused by an excess of wind, bile, or phlegm. It also increases the power of digestion.

IX. Lie upon the back on the floor at full length like a corpse, keeping the head on a level with the body. This *Âsana* removes fatigue and brings rest and calmness of mind.

The student of Hatha Yoga, having perfected himself in controlling some of these postures, should next take up the breathing exercises. He should carefully study the science of breathing in all its aspects. Posture No. I is one of the easiest and best

Âsanas for one who wishes to control the breath. It favors a tranquil circulation and slow respiration.

A beginner should first practice abdominal breathing through both nostrils, keeping a measured time for inspiration and expiration. Gradually he should be directed by his master to hold the breath in and out. Practicing this internal and external suspension of breath for a few weeks, he should next take up alternate breathing. He may inspire through the left nostril for four seconds and expire through the right for four seconds, then reverse the order, breathing in through the right and out through the left. The alternate breathing exercises will purify the nerves and will make the student well-fitted for higher breathing exercises. The student should then breathe in through one nostril for four seconds, hold the breath counting sixteen seconds, and breathe out through the other nostril counting eight seconds. This exercise, if practiced regularly for three months, will generate new nerve-currents and develop the healing power that is latent in the system.

The Yogi who wishes to cure organic trouble or disease of any kind, should combine the higher breathing exercises with the different postures of the body which bear direct relation to the disturbed organ. He should arouse the healing power stored up at the base of the spine and direct it to the diseased part.

Hatha Yoga describes various methods for cleansing the internal organs. Some of them are extremely beneficial to those who suffer from chronic headache, or cold in the head, catarrh, dyspepsia, or insomnia.

The drinking of cold water through the nose removes headache or chronic cold in the head. A Hatha Yogi cleanses the passage between the nose and the mouth by passing soft cords of delicate thread through the nostrils and bringing them out at the mouth. He can pass the cord through one nostril and bring it out through the other. This purifies the head, makes the sight keen, and removes disease in the parts above the shoulders.

A Hatha Yogi cleanses the alimentary canal by swallowing a long piece of fine muslin three inches wide. He purges the impurities of the intestines by drawing water through the opening at the lower extremity of the alimentary canal. This he does with the help of breathing exercises without using any instrument. Then shaking the water by the alternate exercise of the rectimuscles of the abdomen, he throws out the water through the same passage. An expert Yogi can wash the whole of the alimentary canal by drinking a large quantity of water and letting it pass through the opening at the lower extremity. Thus he becomes free from stomach or intestinal disorder. These exercises are especially recommended for those who are flabby, phlegmatic, or corpulent.

He cures insomnia by assuming posture No. IX, at the same time taking a few deep breaths and holding them after each inspiration.

A Hatha Yogi can swallow his tongue. It is said that he who can swallow his upturned tongue is freed from old age and death, conquers sleep, hunger and thirst, and rises above time. The powers of a perfect Hatha Yogi are indeed wonderful.

He can do and undo anything at his will. He is the master of all physical laws.

Thus we see that perfect health and longevity are the immediate results of the Hatha Yoga practices. To the real seeker after Absolute Truth, however, they have small value except as they become a means of attaining superconscious realization. According to him, if a man lives five hundred years and yet in that time does not reach the state of God-consciousness, he is little better than an oak tree which may outlast many generations and grow to great size, but is in the end only an oak tree. That man, on the contrary, who dies at the age of thirty, having realized his oneness with Divinity, has achieved infinitely more than he who possesses perfect health, longevity, psychic powers, or the gift of healing; for he has become a living God in this world and can point the way of salvation to all mankind. Therefore the exercises of Hatha Yoga should be practiced only so far as the earnest truth-seeker does not attain Râja Yoga, which alone will lead the soul to God-consciousness and perfect freedom.

Râja Yoga

HATHA YOGA, as we have already seen, is wholly devoted to the control of the functions of the body and to the mastery of the physical forces, its ideal being a sound constitution, well-fitted to overcome those physical and environmental conditions which stand as obstacles in the path of spiritual progress. Râja Yoga, on the contrary, deals entirely with the mind and psychic power and may be called the science of applied psychology. Its aim is to remove all mental obstructions and to gain a perfectly controlled, healthy mind. The main purpose of its training is to develop and strengthen the will as well as the power of concentration, and to lead the seeker after Truth through the path of concentration and meditation to the ultimate goal of all religion.

This path is called Râja Yoga or the Royal method (Râja means "king") because the power of concentration and will-power are not only greater than any physical force, but are essential to the acquisition of all other powers. The man who possesses a vigorous mind controlled by a well-developed will, with strong power of concentration, can easily become the master of physical nature and in a short time attain the realization of Truth; and it is the special province of Râja Yoga to teach how this can be accomplished. Its study has been encouraged by all those who have come in contact with the Râja Yogis of India either in ancient or modern times. It was extolled by Pythagoras, by Plato and the Neo-Platonists like Plotinus and Proclus, by the Gnostics and the Christian mystics of the middle ages; and even to-day it is in some measure practiced by some of the Roman Catholic monks and nuns of the higher orders. Spinoza, Kant, Schopenhauer, Ralph Waldo Emerson, spoke in praise of it, declaring its object to be the unravelling of the mystery of the nature of the human soul and the unfoldment of the latent powers existing in each individual. It has been proved by the living example of Yogis that through its practice that power can be acquired by which all other forces in the universe may be controlled; and Râja Yoga claims that whoever has gained mastery over his mind, can govern all the phenomena of nature.

It teaches that mind is the sovereign power of the universe, and that when its forces are properly concentrated upon any particular object, the true nature of that object will be revealed. Instead of using an instrument, if we properly utilize the mental powers which we already possess, and focus them absolutely upon one point, we can easily know all the particulars regarding the thing upon which they are directed. This object may be physical, mental, or spiritual. The concentrated mind of a Yogi may be compared to an electric search-light. By throwing the converged rays of his mind toward a distant object, whether gross or subtile, all the details of that object are illumined and made known to him. The vision of ordinary persons is not so penetrating because their mental forces are dissipated like the scattered rays of an ordinary light In the same way, if the mind can be concentrated upon internal objects or upon truths that exist in the realm of the universal, perfect knowledge of those things can be acquired.

Thus it becomes evident that the power

of concentration is greater than sense-power, or than that which can be gained by the help of instruments. If we can develop it by controlling our mental faculties, by making the mind introspective, and by checking all distractions which draw the mind outside; and can direct our concentrated mental energy toward our higher Self, the true nature of the individual ego will be revealed, and we shall realize that our immutable Self is the Soul of all, and that it is the same as the ultimate Reality of the universe. We shall then perceive that the Divine Being, whom in ignorance we worship as separate from ourselves, is not far from us, is not dwelling outside of us, but is our own omnipotent Self residing within us. We shall also recognize that the same Spirit is one and all-pervading, and that it is the Absolute Truth underlying the name and form of every phenomenal object. This knowledge will emancipate the soul from the bondage of ignorance.

Râja Yoga maintains that the outer world exists only in relation to the inner nature of each individual. What mind is to itself, the phenomenal world of sense-perception is to the mind. The external is only the reflection of the internal; that which we gain, that which we receive, is only the likeness or reflection of that which we have already given. Mental phenomena are merely the effects of invisible forces, which cannot be discovered by the senses or by any instrument which the human mind can invent. We may try forever to know these finer forces through the medium of our sense-perceptions, but we shall never arrive at any satisfactory result. A Râja Yogi understands this and therefore attaches little value to instruments. He does not depend upon his sense-powers, but endeavors to gain all knowledge through the power of concentration. The science of Râja Yoga gives the various steps which lead to the attainment of this ideal. It explains clearly and scientifically the processes and methods by which concentration can be developed. It does not, however, ask the student to accept anything on hearsay, or to believe anything on the mere authority of scriptures or of writers. But it states certain facts, requests the student to experiment, experience the results, and draw his own conclusions.

There is nothing mysterious in the system of Râja Yoga. On the contrary, it points out the laws which govern so-called mysteries and explains under what conditions the phenomena of mysteries are produced. It shows that so long as the real cause of an event is unknown it appears mysterious to us. Standing upon the solid ground of logic and reason, the science of Râja Yoga unravels the riddles of the universe and directs the individual soul toward the attainment of the final end of all religions. Its principles are highly moral and uplifting. It helps the student to understand the true purpose of life and describes the way by which it may be fulfilled here and now. Râja Yoga tells us that we should not think so much of what will happen after death, but that we should make the best use of the present and unfold the latent powers which we already possess, while it reminds us again and again of the fact that the advancement made in this life will be the foundation of future progress. If we gain or develop certain powers before we die, those powers will not be lost, but will remain with us wherever we go after death; while external possessions, we know, cannot accompany us in the grave. The only things that we can carry out of life are our character, our experience and the knowledge gained therefrom. They are our real possessions; and it is these which Râja Yoga will help us to develop; since its chief object is to mould the character and lead the student to the knowledge of the divine nature of the soul. The methods which it teaches can be practiced without joining any secret organization, but merely by following the directions of a true Râja Yogi, who is pure and simple, whose mind is free from doubts, and who is unattached to the objects of the phenomenal plane.

The practice of Râja Yoga is divided into eight steps. The first four are the same as those of Hatha Yoga. The first and second, Yama and Niyama, include all the ethical laws that govern our moral nature. The strict observance of these laws is necessary to the practice of the other steps of Râja Yoga. All the fundamental principles of ethics expounded by Buddha and all the truths proclaimed in the Sermon on the Mount are contained in these first two steps. A beginner in the practice of Râja Yoga should live a strictly moral and pure life, otherwise he will not advance in this path, nor will he reach the highest Truth or realize the Divinity that dwells within him. A neophyte must remember that purity, chastity, and morality are the very corner-stones of the structure of the Science of Yoga. In the requirements of the first step we find non-killing, non-stealing, truthfulness, continence, forgivingness, firmness of character, kindness to all living creatures, simplicity, moderation in diet, and cleanliness. Non-killing must be in thought, word, and deed, so with truthfulness and non-stealing. The character must be firm, for the student must persist in the face of all obstacles until spiritual perfection is reached. He must not take up the study as a passing fad, only to satisfy his momentary curiosity, but must continue with patience and perseverance until the highest ideal is realized.

The second step includes austerities, forbearance, contentment, faith in the Supreme Being, charity, study, and self-surrender to the Divine will. All the physical exercises necessary for keeping the body in perfect condition are to be found in the third step.* Health is essential to the attainment of the highest knowledge. Those who are suffering from disease can-

* It is called *Âsana* in Sanskrit. It has been described more fully in the chapter on Hatha Yoga.

not make their mind steady, cannot fix their attention upon truths existing on the spiritual plane, because naturally their minds will be centered on the diseased parts of the body. A beginner, who possesses a healthy body and a well-balanced mind, should choose any *Âsana* or posture of the body in which he can sit firmly for a long time without feeling pain in the limbs. In the practice of Râja Yoga, however, one need not be so particular regarding the posture of the body. The student should simply observe that the spinal column is kept perfectly straight while practicing breathing lessons in a sitting posture.

Prânâyâma, or breathing exercises, constitute the fourth step. The practice of certain breathing exercises will remove many obstacles like dullness, laziness, and bodily weakness, and will be helpful in gaining control over the senses, sense organs, and nerve centers, as also in quieting the restlessness of the mind. Anyone who will practice such breathing exercises regularly, will acquire wonderful power over both his mind and his body. He who suffers from worry, anxiety, nervousness, or insomnia, can obtain excellent results even in a few days by the practice of proper breathing exercises. Those who have studied the science of breathing will know what these results are; but the main object of the Prânâyâma in Râja Yoga is to develop the power of concentration.

Making the mind introspective is the fifth step. It is called Pratyâhâra. If we can withdraw the mind from external objects, fix it on some inner object, and bring it under the control of the will, we shall accomplish all that is required in this step. Pratyâhâra is preparatory to concentration. Before the student is able to concentrate on any particular object he must learn to gather up his scattered mental powers. This process of collecting the powers of the mind and of restraining it from going out to external objects is what the Yogis designate as Pratyâhâra.

Concentration follows next. After going through the five preliminary steps, if one takes up concentration, the results achieved will be extraordinary. Those, however, who have not practiced the introductory steps will find this one extremely difficult, for the ground must be prepared before good results can be gained.

Meditation is the seventh stage,* and through it one passes into Samâdhi or the state of superconsciousness, which is the

* For further explanations concerning concentration and meditation, see "Spiritual Unfoldment," by the same author.

eighth and last step. In this state the sixth sense of finer perception is developed, the spiritual eye is opened, and one comes face to face with the Divine Being dwelling within. In it the student realizes that his true Self is one with the universal Spirit, and he receives all the revelation and all the inspiration that can possibly come to the human soul. It may be thought by many that revelation proceeds from some external source, either through the favor of some angel or bright spirit or the extra-cosmic personal God, but a Yogi knows that revelation or inspiration is the disclosure of the higher Self within, and that the realization of spiritual truths comes to that soul which has reached the eighth step of Râja Yoga. Ceaseless effort, persistence, and perseverance in practice are necessary to attain to the state of superconsciousness. That which is realized in it cannot be revealed by intellect or by any other mental faculty; therefore it is said that Truth cannot be attained by reading books or Scriptures, or by intellect or sense-perception, but by reaching the state of superconsciousness. Those who are longing to know the Truth, who are searching for the ultimate Reality of the universe, and are not satisfied with the knowledge gained through the senses or through the aid of instruments, should struggle hard to go into Samâdhi, because through it alone will they discover their ideal and reach the abode of happiness. Before, however, they can arrive at this state, they will have to follow faithfully the different steps already enumerated and with patience and perseverance overcome all the obstacles which beset the way.

There are many obstructions to Samâdhi, such as grief, disease, mental laziness, doubt, cessation of the struggle to attain Samâdhi, heaviness of body and mind, thirst for worldly things, false knowledge, non-attaining concentration, falling away from the state once attained, irregular breathing, etc. They can be easily avoided by regular practice under the guidance of a Yogi teacher. If a student try to practice by himself any of the exercises as given in Râja Yoga,* he may have some unpleasant experiences which may disturb his mind or nervous system; but if he have an experienced Râja Yogi to direct him, then he will have no difficulty in conquering all the obstacles and dangers, and in reaching the right destination. Some of the powers generated by these practices are too dangerous to be handled by an inexperienced student; they may not only

* See "Râja Yoga," by Swâmi Vivekânanda. Published by The Baker and Taylor Co., New York.

injure him but may even drive him to insanity. There have, indeed, been many such cases among those who have tried to practice without the help of a well-qualified Guru or spiritual teacher.

Having removed all obstructions in this path, the student should be confident that he is approaching the final goal of Râja Yoga. When the superconscious realization is acquired all doubts will cease forever, all questions concerning the nature of the soul will be answered, the search after Truth will stop, the mind will become tranquil, and the soul will be emancipated from the bondage of ignorance and self-delusion. The Yogi will never again fall a victim to the attractions of the world or be distracted by objects of sense. The whole universe will appear to him as the playground of the Divine Being; and he will constantly feel that his body and mind are like instruments moving under the direction of the Almighty Will which is manifesting through all forms. Thus, having gained spiritual strength and illumination, he will become the conqueror of himself and the master of nature even in this life.

" He alone has reached happiness on this earth, he alone has conquered the world, who has gained perfect control over his mind and body, whose soul rests in tranquillity, and whose eyes behold Divinity in everything and everything in that Eternal Being, which is the Infinite Abode of existence, knowledge, and bliss absolute."

Karma Yoga

ONE of the significations of the word "Yoga" is "Dexterity in work." To render this meaning still more specific, the Sanskrit term "Karma," derived from the root verb "Kri," to act, is added. Taken in its literal sense, therefore, Karma signifies action, and refers to all actions whether of mind or body. Wherever there is activity of any kind, it is Karma. In this sense devotion, love, worship, meditation, concentration, discrimination are all Karma; as are also, for the same reason, eating, drinking, walking, talking, or performing any organic function.

Again, every action, as we are aware, is followed by reaction. No action can be separated from its result, as no cause can be absolutely disconnected from its effect.

Consequently the secondary meaning of Karma embraces all reactions or results of actions. The chain of cause and sequence, known as the "law of causation," is also called Karma; and every action of body and mind is governed by the law of Karma or of action and reaction. Being subject to this natural law, we have been working in this world from the beginningless past, and reaping the results of our efforts, whether pleasant or unpleasant, good or evil.

When, furthermore, we consider that the effect of each action leaves its impression on the mind-substance, which impression becomes the seed of a fresh action of a similar nature, we understand the third meaning of the term. In this sense the word Karma includes the accumulated results of past actions or rather the seed forms of future activities.

Hence the character of an individual, which is the aggregate result of the works of his previous life may be called Karma. In the same way, the future life will be the sum-total of the results of the mental and physical actions of the present life.

Karma Yoga is, therefore, that branch of the Science of Yoga which discusses the three ideas conveyed by the word "Karma," explains the philosophy of work, describes the method by which the individual soul can extricate itself from the wheel of action and reaction, and having escaped from the irresistible law of causation by which every one is bound, can attain to perfect freedom, fulfill the highest purpose of life, and thus through right action alone reach the ultimate goal of all religion. It is the path best fitted for those who believe in no creed, who are not devotional, and who do not care to worship or pray to a personal God.

Karma Yoga teaches that the cause of the suffering, misery, disease, and misfortune, which overshadow our earthly life, lies in our own actions. We reap the fruit of that which we ourselves have sown. These causes are within us. We should blame neither our parents nor any evil spirit for our sufferings, but should look within ourselves to discover the source thereof. This branch of Yoga likewise describes the secret of work, by knowing which we can remove all causes of bondage and suffering, and enjoy freedom, peace, and happiness both here and after death. It tells us that every action inspired by the motive of desire for results attaches the soul to these results, and consequently becomes a source of bondage. The secret of work consists in working for work's sake and not for fruits. If this principle be applied to the actions of our daily lives, then every work done by us will help us to advance toward the perfect emancipation of the soul. Whoever performs his duties understanding the secret of work, becomes truly unselfish and eventually gains knowledge of his real Self, which is immortal and divine.

According to Karma Yoga, the true Self when it becomes identified with the limitations of the mind and the physical form, appears as "ego," "doer," or "actor," and performing work from various motives, remains attached to its results. We thus feel as one with our body and endeavor to enrich the narrow, limited self or "I" by getting something from that which is "not I." This imperfect knowledge of the "Self," or rather this ignorance of the true "Self," is the cause of selfishness.

From selfishness in turn proceeds all that desire for results which forces us to live and act like slaves. Karma Yoga shows us the way by which we can become conscious of our true Self, and, by widening the range of the limited "ego," can make it universal. When we have accomplished this, we shall live in the world working not from selfish motives, but for humanity, yet with as much interest in heart as we had when we worked for ourselves. Nor shall we then seek the comfort and pleasure of this little personality which is now the chief center of our interest and effort, but shall strive for the good of all.

Anyone who wishes to become a true Karma Yogi should clearly understand the philosophy of work, * and should remember that every action of body and mind must produce some effect which will event-

* See "Philosophy of Work," by the same author.

ually come back upon the doer; and that, if there be the smallest desire for result, it will be the seed of future action of a like nature. He should also realize that every action produces similar reaction. If the action be in harmony with the moral and physical laws which govern our lives, then the reaction which comes back upon the actor will bring only that which is good,—peace, rest, fortune, health, and happiness. If, on the contrary, these laws are violated, then the result will be evil, producing restlessness, discomfort, loss of fortune, disease, and unhappiness.

A traveller in the path of Karma Yoga should not even think evil of another, because in the attempt to injure others we first injure ourselves. Every thought puts the mind-substance in a certain state of vibration and opens the door to the influence of such minds as are in the same state of vibration. Therefore when we cherish evil thoughts, we run the double risk of affecting other minds and of being influenced by all evil-minded persons holding similar thoughts, nay, we expose our minds to all the evil thoughts that have been thought in the past and stored up in the mental atmosphere of the world. A corresponding result comes from the holding of good thoughts. This is the reason why evil-doers grow worse and worse every day, and the doers of good deeds become better and better.

A Karma Yogi should realize that there is one Being, or one Spirit, in the universe. Seeing this same Being or Spirit in all living creatures, he should recognize the rights of all and should not injure anyone either mentally or physically. Such a Yogi is truly unselfish; he is a blessing to the world and to humanity.

He who wishes to practice Karma Yoga should abandon attachment to the fruit of his labors, and learn to work for work's sake, keeping in mind the idea that by his work he is paying off the debt which he owes to parents, to society, to country, and to all mankind. Like a wet nurse he should take care of his children, realizing that they do not belong to him, but that they are placed in his charge in order that he and they may gain experience and unfold their latent powers and feelings.

A true Karma Yogi, furthermore, is he who recognizes that his real Self is not a doer of action, but that all mental and physical activity is merely the result of the forces of nature. Therefore he never claims that any work, whether good or bad, has been done by his true "Self." He lets his mind, intellect, and sense-organs work incessantly, while in his soul he holds steadfastly to the idea that he is the witness-like Knower of all activity, mental or physical. In this way he frees himself from the law of Karma and escapes from all the results of work which bind ordinary workers. Neither does he count success or failure in his daily life. He does his best in each effort put forth by him, and after performing his duty to the utmost of his ability, if he meets with failure he does not grieve, but, saying within himself that he did all that he could under the circumstances, he maintains his calmness and enjoys peace of mind even in the face of defeat.

The aim of a Karma Yogi is to live in the world and act like a master, not like a slave. Ordinary mortals implicitly obey the masters of desire and passion, following them without question or discrimination. But he who chooses the path of Karma Yoga seeks absolute control over desire and passion and directs the force manifesting through these channels toward the highest ideal of life—freedom of the soul.

In fulfilling all the duties of life the Karma Yogi takes refuge in love, making it the sole motive power behind every action of body and mind; and whenever he performs any duty, it is always through love. He understands that sense of duty is bondage, while work done through a feeling of love frees the soul and brings peace, rest, and, in the end, everlasting happiness.

All the great spiritual leaders of mankind, like Christ and Buddha, were Karma Yogis. They worked for humanity through love, and showed by their example how perfect freedom can be attained by right work. Buddha did not preach the worship of a personal God, but he established the truth that those who do not believe in a personal God and who are not devotional, can reach the highest goal of all religions by the path of Karma Yoga.

Bhakti Yoga

BHAKTI YOGA teaches that the final end of all religions can be reached through love and worship of the personal God, who is the Creator and Governor of the phenomenal universe. It leads to the same destination as all the other branches of Yoga, but is especially suited for such as are emotional in their nature and have the feeling of love and devotion highly developed. It is for those devotees who, conscious of their own weakness arising from lack of self-control and of knowledge, seek help from outside; and who, taking refuge in the Supreme, pray to Him for forgiveness and for pardon of sins committed through ignorance of the moral and spiritual laws that govern our lives.

All dualistic systems of religion, like Christianity, Judaism, and Mahometanism, which advocate the worship of a personal God, knowingly or unknowingly preach Bhakti Yoga and direct their adherents along this path.

The word "Bhakti" means devotion, while Yoga in this case signifies union of the individual soul with God. Hence Bhakti Yoga is the method of devotion by which true communion of the soul with the Supreme Deity is accomplished. It shows what kind of devotion and love for God will bring the soul into the most intimate relation with the Divine Being; and how even the ordinary feelings of a human heart, when directed Godward, can become the means of attaining spiritual oneness with the Soul of the universe. Râja Yoga tells us that desire, passion, love, hatred, pride, anger, must be completely conquered before perfection can be reached. A student of Râja Yoga must not only keep constant watch over his mind, but he must also faithfully practice the eight steps already described, if he would achieve his highest ideal; while in Bhakti Yoga we learn that all desires and passions, whether good or bad, can be directed towards God. Then, instead of binding the soul to worldliness and earthly attachment, they become a means of attaining God-consciousness and absolute freedom from selfishness and wickedness.

A follower of Bhakti Yoga should feel God as closely related to his soul as he possibly can; and regard Him not only as the Lord of the universe, but as father, mother, brother, sister, friend, or child. Even the relation existing between husband and wife may be cultivated and developed in the heart of a lover of

God, intoxicated by the soul-stirring wine of Divine Love. When the whole heart and soul of a Bhakta or lover of God flow like the unbroken current of a mighty river, surmounting all barriers and dashing headlong toward the ocean of Divinity, he finds no other attraction in the world, holds no other thought, cherishes no other desire, speaks no other word, and sees no other thing than his most Beloved, the Omnipresent Deity. He resigns himself entirely to Him and surrenders his will to the will of the Almighty One. He works, but without thinking of results. Every action of his body and mind is performed simply to please his Beloved One. His motive power is love alone and by this he breaks asunder the chain of selfishness, transcends the law of Karma, and becomes free. Thus a true Bhakti Yogi, being constantly in tune with the Infinite, loses the sense of "I," "Me," and "Mine," and makes room for "Thou," "Thee," and "Thine."

A Bhakta never forgets his relation to his Beloved. His mind is concentrated and one-pointed; consequently meditation becomes easy for him. True devotion or continuous remembrance of the Divine Ideal leads to unceasing meditation, and ultimately lifts the soul into Samâdhi, where it realizes God and communes with Him undisturbed by any other thought, feeling, idea, or sensation. Becoming dead to sense phenomena, it lives on the spiritual plane of God-consciousness. Wherever such a Yogi casts his eyes, he sees the presence of the All-pervading Divinity and enjoys unbounded peace and happiness at every moment of his life. It is for this reason that Bhakti Yoga is considered to be the easiest of all methods. What a Râja Yogi attains only after years of practice, a Bhakta accomplishes in a short time through extreme devotion and love. That which a Karma Yogi finds so difficult to achieve, a Bhakti Yogi attains easily by offering the fruits of all his works to the Almighty Source of all activity and the ultimate end of all motives.

Bhakti Yoga has two grades,—the first is called "Gauni," or preparatory and includes all the preliminary practices; the second is "Parâ," or the state of supreme love and devotion to God. A beginner in Bhakti Yoga should first of all prepare the ground of his heart by freeing it from attachment to earthly objects and sense-pleasures; then by arousing in it extreme longing to see God, to realize Divinity, to go to the Source of all knowledge, and to reach perfection and God-consciousness in this life. He must be absolutely earnest and sincere. He should seek the company of a true lover of God, whose life is pure and spotless, who has renounced all worldly connections, and who has realized the true relation which the individual soul bears to the Universal Spirit. If, by good fortune, he meets such a real Bhakta, he should receive from him the seed of Bhakti, plant it in the ground of his heart, and by faithfully following the instructions of the master, take special care to keep it alive and make it grow, until it becomes a large tree bearing the fruit of Divine Love. He should have respect, reverence, and love for his master, who will open his spiritual eye and transmit his own spiritual powers to his soul. When these powers begin to work, the soul will be awakened from the deep sleep of ignorance and self-delusion.

The Guru, or spiritual eye-opener, knowing the natural tendency of the disciple, will advise him to look upon God as his Master, or as his Father or Mother, and will thus establish a definite relation between his soul and God. Henceforth the disciple should learn to worship or pray to the Supreme through this particular relation. At this stage symbols, rituals, ceremonies may appeal to his mind; or he may repeat some name of the Lord that signifies the special aspect of the Divinity corresponding to the relation which he bears to Him. Constant repetition of such a name will help the mind of the neophyte to become concentrated upon the Divine Being. During this period he should avoid such company, such places, and such amusements as make him forget his chosen Ideal. He should live a chaste and pure life, always discriminating right from wrong and struggling to control his passions and desires by directing them Godward. He should be angry with himself for not realizing his ideal; he should hate his sinful nature because it keeps him away from the path of Bhakti and prevents him from remembering his Beloved. Thus he will gradually succeed in correcting his faults and in gaining control over his animal nature.

A traveller on the path of Bhakti should observe cleanliness of body and mind, should be truthful, and lead a simple life, without injuring any living creature mentally or physically. He should not kill any animal for his food, neither should he covet that which does not belong to him. He should, furthermore, obey the laws of health which tend to make him physically strong, as well as those moral laws the violation of which weakens the mind.

So long as the devotee thinks of God

with a form and believes that He is outside of his soul and of the universe, he can make a mental picture of Him and worship the Divine Ideal through that form; or he may keep before him some symbolic figure like the cross which will remind him of his Ideal at the time of devotion. But a Bhakta should never mistake the imaginary form or the symbolic figure for the real Ideal. Wherever there is such a mistake there is to be found spiritual degeneration and the expression of ignorance in the form of sectarianism, bigotry, fanaticism.

Gradually, as the Bhakti approaches God, he will rise above such dualistic conceptions and realize that his Beloved is not only transcendent but immanent in nature, that nature is His body, that He dwells everywhere, that He is the Soul of our souls and the Life of our life, that He is the one stupendous Whole while we are but

His parts. The Bhakta then reaches that state which is called qualified non-dualism. He sees that from the minutest insect up to man all living creatures are related to the Iswara * as a part is related to the whole. Therefore he cannot kill or injure any living being. Understanding that everything pertaining to any part belongs in reality to the whole, he says, "Whatever is mine is Thine"; and it is from this moment that absolute self-resignation and self-surrender to the will of the Iswara begin to reign supreme in the soul of the Yogi. Then he is able to say from the bottom of his heart, "Let Thy will be done," and never again can he forget that his soul is a part of the Iswara. His devotion henceforth consists in remembering this new relation, and his

* The most appropriate Sanskrit word for God who is the all-pervading, internal Ruler of the universe.

worship takes a new form. Whatever he does with mind or body becomes an act of worship of the Supreme Whole, for he realizes that he possesses no power that does not belong to God. Eating, drinking, walking, talking, and every other work of his daily life become acts of devotion, and the entire existence of such a Bhakta is a continuous series of acts of worship. Then the heart is purified and selfishness is dead.

The devotee thus rises to the second grade of Bhakti Yoga and begins to taste that Divine Love which is the fruit of the tree of Bhakti. Here all distinction between lover and Beloved disappears; the lover, the Beloved and Love all merge into one ocean of Divinity. The soul of the Bhakta is transformed, and manifesting omniscience, God-consciousness, perfect freedom, and all other Divine qualities, it attains to the highest ideal of Bhakti Yoga.

Jnâna Yoga

THE last is Jnâna Yoga, the path of wisdom. The word "Jnâna," being derived from the Sanskrit root "Jnâ," to know, means knowledge; and the ideal which it holds up before its followers is the realization of that Absolute Truth, which is the one common source of all subjective and objective phenomena in the universe. It teaches that there is one life, one Being, one Reality, and that all notions of distinction and differentiation, that all beliefs in the permanent duality or multiplicity of existence are unreal and illusory.

Jnâna Yoga is based entirely upon the monistic principles of the *Advaita* or non-dualistic system of Vedânta. Its purpose is to show that subject and object are but the two expressions of one Absolute Being or Substance; that God and man, the Creator and the created, are only different aspects of one Universal Reality. Its aim is to resolve the divers phenomena into one ultimate Being, from which proceed all powers and all forces manifested in external and internal nature, and which is the abode of infinite intelligence and eternal happiness.

According to Jnâna Yoga, matter, mind, intellect, sense-powers, names, and forms are but the apparent manifestations of that one Substance which is called in Sanskrit *Brahman*. They may appear to us as real, but they have in truth only relative reality. The phenomena of the universe are like the waves in the ocean of Brahman. As waves rise in the sea, and after playing for a while, once more merge into it, so the waves of subject and object rise, live, and dissolve in the ocean of that Absolute Substance Brahman. Brahman is described in Vedânta as "That of which all animate and inanimate objects are born, by which they live, and into which they return after dissolution. It should be known and realized by all." It is the essence of Divinity. It is like the eternal canvas upon which the Creator or the Cosmic Ego and the created or individual egos are painted by Mâyâ, the inscrutable creative power of the Infinite Being.

The chief object of Jnâna Yoga is to unify God and the individual Soul and to show the absolute oneness that exists between them on the highest spiritual plane. The individual ego; being the reflection or image of Divinity or Brahman, in its true nature is divine, and this true Self is known in Sanskrit as the *Âtman*. The knowledge of this oneness of the Âtman or subjective reality with Brahman, the Universal Truth, is described in Jnâna Yoga as the only means of attaining to complete liberation from the bondage of selfishness and from attachment to body and senses, which are the causes of all worldliness, unhappiness, and misery. The light of the knowledge of the Âtman and of its unity with Brahman alone will dispel the darkness of ignorance which prevents us from reaching the abode of Absolute Existence, Intelligence, and Bliss, and which now deludes us into identifying the individual Self with the body, senses, mind, and their modifications. This ignorance is designated in Sanskrit *Avidyâ* or ne-science, and is the source of all false knowledge, egotism, attachment to the lower self and to the world. Being deceived by the illusive power of *Avidyâ,* we mistake body for soul and soul for body, matter for spirit and spirit for matter. In ignorance of our true Self, we work solely to gratify selfish motives and to reap some result from our actions. But Jnâna Yoga would waken us from this sleep of ignorance, by showing us that the Âtman is immortal, unchangeable, all-knowing, and free by its own nature from eternity to eternity; that through the influence of *Avidyâ*, the individual ego thinks of itself as changeable and subject to birth and death, and forgetting that the fountain-head of freedom, knowledge, and everlasting happiness is abiding within, it seeks knowledge and happiness from outside and becomes the slave of desires and passions. It further reminds us that whatever we think or perform mentally or physically is like a dream in the sleep of self-delusion caused by the power of *Avidyâ;* that these dreams of the sleep of ignorance can be removed neither by work, nor by devotion, nor by meditation, but by the light and power of *Vidyâ*, the knowledge of the Âtman or Self and of its relation to Brahman.

This knowledge cannot be obtained as the result of any virtuous act or prayer, but comes to the soul when the intellect and heart have been purified by unselfish and righteous works, and when the individual ego begins to discriminate between the real and unchangeable Âtman and apparent and changeable matter or force. Jnâna Yoga teaches that right discrimination and proper analysis are indispensable to the acquisition of knowledge of the true Self and of the Reality which underlies phenomenal objects. It also declares that knowledge of the Self will bring to the soul the realization of Absolute Truth more quickly than the practice of Râja, Karma, or Bhakti Yoga.

The path of wisdom, therefore, is best fitted for those earnest and sincere seekers after Truth who have no leaning towards active life, who are not devotional in their nature, but who are preëminently intellectual, and who, having realized the transitory and ephemeral character of phenomenal objects, are no longer contented with sense-pleasures. It is for those who wish to be free from all fetters and attachments, and who care nothing for earthly prosperity, success, social honor, fame, or the fulfilment of personal ambitions; but whose sole desire is to know who they are in reality, what is their true nature, and what relation exists between their soul, God, and the universe.

A traveller along this path should be philosophical in tendency, should have a sharp intellect and a keen power of analyzing the true nature of things. He should also have a firm conviction that the ultimate Truth or Reality of the universe is unchangeable. Using the sword of right discrimination between the Self and the non-self, he should sever all ties, and should never allow himself to be overpowered by any external or internal influence. His mind should be undisturbed by passions or desires, his senses well controlled, and his body strong, healthy, and capable of bearing all hardships as well as of overcoming all environmental conditions. He should have dispassion; and be ever ready to renounce anything that does not help him in his realization of Truth. He must have absolute confidence in the teachings of Jnâna Yogins, or those who have become Seers of Truth by following the path of wisdom; and he must likewise have faith in the final Truths expounded by the monistic system of Vedânta.

The mind of a beginner in Jnâna Yoga must possess the power of perfect concentration and meditation; and his soul must be filled with the longing for absolute freedom from all relative conditions and from the laws which govern phenomena. He must realize that even the enjoyment of heavenly pleasures is a kind of bondage, since it keeps the soul entangled in the meshes of phenomenal relativity. Being well-armed with all these noble qualities as his weapons, a Jnâna Yogi should fight against phenomenal appearances, and with the ideal of the unity of the true Self and the Absolute Brahman ever before his mind's eye, he should march onward toward its realization, breaking down all names and forms with the hammer of right analysis, and cleaving all ties of attachment with the sword of proper discrimination. Nor should he stop until the goal is reached. He who goes through the path of wisdom, burns the vast forest of the trees of phenomenal names and forms by starting in it the fire of right knowledge. All these names and forms are produced by Mâyâ, the inscrutable power of Brahman; and according to Jnâna Yoga this power of Mâyâ is inseparable from Brahman as the power of heating is inseparable from fire. A Jnâna Yogi, in his search after Brahman, should reject all names and forms by saying "Not this," "Not this," until he realizes the one nameless, formless, and absolute Being of the universe, where the subject and the object, the knower, knowledge, and its object, losing their relativity, merge into the infinite Ocean of Blissful Existence and Supreme Intelligence.

A sincere seeker after Truth should hear over and over again that the Âtman or true Self is one with Brahman or the Eternal Truth; and should repeat such phrases as "I am Brahman," "I am one with the Absolute Source of knowledge, existence, and bliss." He should constantly think of the meaning of "*Tat Twam asi*"—"That thou art," and should devote his time to meditating upon this oneness until the light of Brahman illumines his soul, dispelling the darkness of *Avidyâ* and transforming his ego into the essence of Divinity.

Instead of worshipping a personal God like a Bhakta, a Jnâna Yogi should clearly understand the true significance of all His attributes as given in the different Scriptures—such as Creator or Governor of the universe, He is Spirit, infinite, omniscient, all-powerful, unchangeable, true, and one; and rejecting the worship of the personal God as an act proceeding from *Avidyâ* or ignorance of the divine nature of the Self or Âtman, he should seek that which is above all attributes and beyond all descriptions, which transcends the realm of thought and cannot be revealed by human intellect or understanding. He should realize that all conceptions of a personal God are more or less anthropomorphic, and that the Creator himself must be phenomenal since He can exist only in relation to the created object. A Jnâna Yogi, consequently, does not pray to the personal God or to any other Spirit or Being. To him prayers and devotions are useless and unnecessary. He does not seek any supernatural help or Divine mercy, for he is conscious of the omnipotent and omniscient nature of the Âtman, and knows that his true Self is beyond good and evil, above virtue and vice, unlimited by all laws, and that it reigns over nature in its own glory.

He feels that it is the same in essence as the Creator or personal God. Instead of identifying himself with body, mind, senses, or intellect, he always remembers that he is the Âtman, which is birthless, deathless, sinless, fearless, immutable, eternally peaceful, and ever undisturbed by pleasant or unpleasant experiences, sensations, or mental and physical changes.

A true Jnâna Yogi constantly tries to keep himself above all phenomenal conditions, and incessantly repeats "I am Brahman," "Soham"—I am He, I am He. He says within himself:

"I am neither mind, nor intellect, nor ego, nor senses; I am neither earth, nor water, nor air, nor fire, nor ether, but my true nature is absolute existence, knowledge, and bliss. I am He, I am He."

"I am neither the organic activity nor am I the elements of the body, neither the sense of knowledge nor that of action, but I am absolute existence, knowledge, and bliss. I am He, I am He."

"I have neither hatred nor love, neither greed nor delusion, neither egotism nor pride nor vanity, neither creed nor faith, nor aim nor desire for freedom. I am absolute existence, knowledge, and bliss. I am He, I am He."

"I have neither virtue nor vice nor sin, neither pleasure nor pain, neither Scriptures nor rituals nor ceremonies. I am neither food nor am I the eater. I am absolute existence, knowledge, and bliss. I am He, I am He."

"I have neither death nor fear of death, nor birth nor caste distinction; neither father nor mother, neither friend nor foe, neither master nor disciple. I am absolute existence, knowledge, and bliss. I am He, I am He."

"I have neither doubt nor question. I am formless and all-pervading. I am the eternal Lord of nature and the master of the senses. I am neither bound nor free. I am one with Brahman. I am the omnipresent Divinity, I am the immutable Lord of all. I am absolute existence, knowledge, and bliss. I am He, I am He."

Thus constantly practicing discrimination and rising above all relativity and phenomenal appearances, a Jnâna Yogi realizes the Absolute, Unchangeable, Eternal Truth in this life and ultimately becomes one with it; because Jnâna Yoga declares that he who knows Brahman becomes Brahman, for the same reason that the knower of God can be no other than God himself. A Jnâna Yogi never forgets that his true Self is Brahman. Having attained to this supreme God-consciousness, he lives in the world like an eternal witness of all mental and physical changes. Ever happy and undisturbed, he travels from place to place, pointing out to mankind the way to absolute freedom and perfection. A perfect Jnâna Yogi, indeed, lives as the embodiment of the Absolute Divinity on this earth.

Science of Breathing

Science of Breathing

THE Science of Yoga with its various branches justly claims, as we have already seen, to unravel the mysteries of life and death. Some of the advanced thinkers in Western countries are beginning to understand the importance of this noble science and to explain the problems of existence by it; but modern physiologists, anatomists, biologists, and medical practitioners are still uncertain as to the proper solution of these problems; the more they investigate, the more doubts arise in their minds. Within the last fifty years the various researches in the different departments of science, such as physics, chemistry, physiology, and biology, have apparently ended in the conclusion that life is nothing but the result of physical and chemical actions in the organic structure, that there is no such thing as vital force distinct and separate from the physical and chemical forces which have been discovered in the scientist's laboratory.

Some of the students of science are even anxiously waiting in the vain expectation that some day they will hear of the discovery of a substance, artificially produced in the laboratory, which will live, move, grow, multiply, and die like a particle of living matter. The majority of modern thinkers, in fact, hold that vitality is merely the result of the mechanical activity of the organs; that life comes directly from dead matter, and obeys physical, chemical, and mechanical laws; that a living animal is nothing but a machine; and that all of his actions whether of body or mind are purely mechanical. They say that a living protoplasm is only a combination of certain chemical elements, subject to ordinary chemical laws; that living and non-living are one; and that the living comes directly from the non-living. According to these scientists a human being is no more than a mechanical resultant of certain chemical changes governed by the laws of physical nature. If, however, we ask them what force it is that determines these physical and mechanical modifications, what is the power that causes all these chemical changes in such numberless varieties, they answer that they do not know.

Are we really like machines, subject to mechanical laws and nothing more? Is our growth entirely due to the process of accretion and aggregation of matter in the non-living world? Are we merely some accidental precipitation, deposition, or crystallization of atoms and molecules which are governed by no power higher than the chemico-physical forces? Students of physiology now learn in their text-books this physico-chemical theory of the origin of life. They laugh at those who use such expressions as "vital energy," "vital force," "vitality," or "life force," in the sense of some power separate and distinct from the physico-chemical forces of nature. In fact, when they study physiology they throw aside all ideas of vitality or life force; they believe in a nature devoid of vitality or life, and try to explain the formation of brain cells, nerves, tissues, and the construction of the various organs of a living animal without recognizing the existence of a vital agency. A reaction, however, has taken place recently in Europe, and a class of scientific thinkers has appeared, Dr. Lionel S. Beale being the most prominent, who, having found no satisfactory explanation of life through these theories, have, after closer observation and experiment, come to the conclusion that there is a vital force entirely distinct from mechanical or physico-chemical forces, and which manifests itself through living particles of matter.

It is true that the human body is a machine, but not like any machine made by man. It is a self-moving, self-regulating, and self-adjusting, vital machine governed by will-power and intelligence. It was produced by a germ of life which possessed vitality, and which had the capability of becoming conscious, of willing, thinking, and producing psychic activity, in which are included all emotions and thoughts belonging to a human being. By a germ of life is meant that germ of matter or substance which contains the potentiality of life and mind. Although the manifestation of this vital force depends upon organic structure, still it is not the same as any of the familiar forces known to us; it is not like heat, electricity, magnetism, or molecular attraction. On the contrary, it is a force which governs and directs all these grosser physical forces. It is the director of the telegraphic current which notifies the energy of the muscle when and how to exert itself. It coördinates all automatic movements, controls the system as a whole as well as in detail, and is itself the principle of purely animal life. The special organ through which it functions chiefly, and which has been constructed to differentiate it from other energies, to give it a form and a purpose, and to afford it a vehicle of expression, is the spinal nerve of the vertebrate and the equivalent organ in other animals.

This mysterious and invisible vital energy or vital force is called in Sanskrit "Prâna." That branch of the Science of Yoga which treats of this mysterious force, describing its origin and nature, and teaching how it can be controlled and utilized to produce wonderful results, is known as the Science of Prâna. Ordinarily it is translated into English by the word "Breath," and called the "Science of Breath"; but Prâna is not simple breath. In the Upanishads it is defined as the cause of all motion and life in both the organic and inorganic worlds. Wherever there is the slightest expression of motion, life, or mind, from the smallest atom, or animalcule, or amœba, or bioplasm, up to the largest solar system and the highest man, it is the manifestation of the all-pervading force called Prâna. It is one, yet appears as manifold through its divers expressions. It is the mother of all forces, psychical, chemical, and physical. Vedânta Philosophy describes it as the ultimate generalization of the multiple forces of nature. It is indestructible; the death of the form through which it manifests cannot destroy it; but it must not be confounded with molecular attraction for it is much finer; it cannot be seen, touched, weighed, measured, or captured by any means.

According to Vedânta, before the beginning of creation the unconditioned causal state of the universe contained potential Prâna; Vedânta does not make the absurd statement that life has come from non-life. It does not admit that vital energy is the result of mechanical forces, but, on the contrary, tells us that it is a force which operates simultaneously with physico-chemical forces. They are all, in fact, expressions of the one living energy of Prâna. Although some of the modern scientific monists acknowledge that all matter and force spring from a common source, or from one eternal energy, still at the same time they deny the existence of life or vitality in that energy and declare that it is not living. They try to prove that life is the product of some kind of motion of dead matter; while Vedânta teaches that all the phenomena of the universe have evolved out of the one eternal substance which possesses Prâna or cosmic vital force, cosmic mind, cosmic intelligence, and consciousness. These may be interdependent, but as they all exist in a human being, so the infinite variety of forces exist in that one eternal living Being whose body is the universe.

The Science of Yoga claims that this Prâna is the final cause of all the manifested forces of nature. Why does an atom move and vibrate? A scientist does not know, but a Yogi says because of Prâna. That force which produces vibration in an atom or a molecule is one of the expressions of the energy of Prâna or the cosmic Life-principle. The same Prâna appears as that power by which a germ of life works on the physical plane, arouses motion in the molecules of its cells and builds up a suitable structure, repairs injuries and reproduces its kind. It causes activity in a protoplasm, in a bioplasm or an amœba, as well as in the highest man. It is closely related to the mind, which includes all the psychic activities and intelligence displayed by that germ in the different grades of its evolution. Vital power and mind are, indeed, two aspects of one Prâna. A germ of life possesses mentality as well as vitality, and the phenomena of these two aspects are most intimately connected with one another. In the science of Yoga the relation between mind and Prâna is described as that of a horse and a rider, Prâna being the horse which the individual mind rides. The body moves like an automobile carriage when it is propelled from within by the force of Prâna and guided by the driver of the intelligent mind. The activity of the mechanism of the body stops if Prâna or vital force ceases to vibrate. Again, when the vibration of Prâna is arrested, the mind no longer operates on the physical plane. It is for this reason that vital force or Prâna is called the medium through which the mind expresses its powers on the physical plane.

The animal organism is nothing but a mechanism for the manifestation of the powers of the soul. When the soul wishes to express certain powers on the material plane it creates through Prâna some suitable organism to fulfill its desire. If the mental activities of any living creature change, the organic structure of the nerves and cells will also change. Various experiments have been made by different scientists which clearly show that mental effort underlies all physiological conditions and organic functions. An abnormal activity of the mind will invariably give rise to certain pathological conditions, because it will affect the vital action; and when the vital power, which gives life to every cell of the body, is influenced, the cells will begin to vibrate in a different manner; and the result will be abnormal activity in the cells of the organs, which in turn will produce various diseases. Conversely, when the vital activity is normal, the psychic function is also natural. The mind is just as much affected by a diseased body as the physical system is disturbed by a diseased mind. He who can regulate his mentalities knows how to preserve his vitality and keep a healthy body; while he who has control over his vital functions understands the secret of keeping a healthy mind. The man who is thus able to dominate both body and mind is the master of himself, the king in his own conscious domain. But he who is not the master of himself lives like a slave to passion, to sense-objects, to wealth, property, ambition, and all earthly desires. Those who do not know how to regulate their vital forces are always unhappy, for they constantly suffer either mentally or physically.

Every irregular activity of the mind will produce chemical and physiological change in the nerve centers, in the organs, and eventually in the whole body. This can be shown by analyzing the chemical properties of the secretions of different organs, and especially by analyzing the breath. If we analyze the breath of a person who is strongly moved by anger or any other violent passion, we shall find that his whole system is poisoned for the time being. By letting his breath pass through a certain solution in a glass tube, we shall readily see that distinct changes are produced in the solution. These variations, furthermore, are only the outward signs of the internal modifications that have taken place in the entire nervous system. It is, in fact, these organic changes that modify the breath; but in a normal, healthy state of mind and body the chemical solution will remain perfectly unchanged. The breathing is then regular, deep, and strong. Every impulse of passion that takes possession of the mind, causes a corresponding variation in the respiratory functions; anger, hatred, or jealousy for instance, are marked by short, quick breath, while thoughts of peace, of true happiness, and of divine love produce long, deep breath.

There are various ways of learning the relation that exists between vital activity and mentality. A Yogi says that all abnormal and diseased conditions of the body are caused directly by imperfect or weak expression of the vital energy, and indirectly by improper mental activity. The curing of a disease, therefore, means the removing of the obstacles which prevent the Prâna from working in an absolutely normal way. This can be done either by physical processes or by regulating the mental functions. A Yogi heals disease in himself by increasing the vital action; by rousing the latent powers of the Prâna, which is the source of all life force. He knows how to fill his whole body, nay, every cell, with increased vitality. By regulating the polarity of the cells through the higher vibrations of Prâna he generates a strong current of vibratory Prâna, directs its course through the disordered cells of his organs, and changes the structure of these cells by creating a rapid circulation of the blood charged with the healing power of Prâna, and sending it to the parts affected. In this way the cells are restored to their normal condition and the disease is cured. The Yogi does this consciously and in the most scientific manner with the help of breathing exercises accompanied by concentration. According to the Science of Yoga all nervous currents and all molecular motion in the brain cells and nerve centers are caused by this Prâna. If the molecules of the cells be filled with a new and strong current of Prâna or vital force, their vibration will be enormously increased; and this will enable them to throw off the impure matter that retarded their natural activity, and recover their normal healthy condition.

The same Prâna is also the propelling power in circulation. A Yogi says that the vital energy is stored up in the nerve centers of the spinal cord. It is the cause of the motion of the lungs, which in turn produces respiration; and respiration is the cause of the circulation of the blood and of all other organic activity. Modern physiology tells us that every portion of our body, every tissue and cell breathes; that the lung is nothing more than an instrument in the respiratory process, the chemical operation, which is the essential part of this function, occurring elsewhere in the cells and tissues themselves. The lung is only the door through which oxygen enters the system. The physiologists of the eighteenth century held quite different views; even the father of modern chemistry, Lavoisier himself (1743–1794), supposed that the main act of respiration took place in the lungs. What really happens is that oxygen, introduced into the lungs, filters through the thin walls of the pulmonary capillaries, where it finds in the red corpuscles of the blood a substance called hemoglobin, with which it unites to form a compound known as oxy-hemoglobin. And a very unstable compound it is, for throughout the tissues, in the capillary vessels of the whole body, oxygen is allowed to escape freely and to effect its work upon the cells. The blood, therefore, is merely a vehicle. The "organic combustions" do not occur in the lungs, their seat being in the cells and tissues throughout the whole system.

Physiological chemistry tells us that all things mineral, vegetable, and animal, are mainly composed of four principal elements—oxygen, hydrogen, carbon, and nitrogen. Of these oxygen is of the greatest importance, since it is the most widely diffused, constituting by weight one-fifth of the atmosphere, eight-ninths of the ocean and all water, nearly one-half of solid rock and of every solid substance, and more than one-half of all vegetables and animals. If a man weighs one hundred and fifty pounds, one hundred and ten of his weight is oxygen. It is the chief cause of all activity in mechanical, chemical, muscular, and mental forces. The amount of energy or activity of an animal is determined by the amount of oxygen he respires; and the degree of force manifested in the human organism is in proportion to the rate at which oxygen is introduced into the system. It is the first requisite of vital action. Without it all other materials of life will be of little avail; and the respiratory organs are the medium through which it enters the system. The blood which has been once used in our bodies would be of no further service if it were not purified by the lungs. Ordinarily air when inhaled, contains 21 per cent oxygen, and when exhaled, 12 per cent, having lost 9 per cent. In a healthy adult man the average pulsation is 75 in a minute and about two ounces of blood are driven by each pulsation from the heart to the lungs, or nine pounds and six ounces in a minute. The quantity of blood in the human body is considered to be about one-fifth of the weight of the entire body, or twenty-eight pounds in a man weighing one hundred and forty pounds. The full quantity of blood in the system will, therefore, flow through the lungs in the short period of three minutes; in other words, the vast amount of thirteen thousand five hundred pounds in every twenty-four hours.

It is well known now that as a rule only one-sixth of the full capacity of the lungs is used; if the remaining five-sixths were properly brought into play who can say what marvellous results might not follow? Nature has not given capacity to any organ without a purpose; and we are sure that, if every one were to use the full capacity of his lungs, weak or diseased lungs would be a thing of the past. If we understand the science of breathing, we can develop our lung power to its utmost capacity; then by well-regulated breathing exercises we can purify every particle of matter in the cells of the organs, and with the help of the current of Prâna can ultimately drive out all physical weakness.

Faith-healers, mental-healers, and Christian Scientists cure disease without giving drugs; the Yogis of India do the same, but in a more scientific manner. Faith-healers and Christian Scientists ask us to believe in a certain thing and to declare that we are not suffering. A Yogi says that we can get better and surer results if through breathing exercises we can control the Prâna, increase the vital current, and fill the whole system with the healing power of Prâna. By polarizing the activity of the cells, and removing the obstacles that prevent the proper manifestation of the vital current in those cells, we shall get rid of the disease. If mental-healers and faith-healers knew the secret of controlling the Prâna, they would have been undoubtedly more successful in their attempts. Some among them are now beginning to take up breathing exercises, and perhaps in time they will learn the truths contained in the wonderful science of breathing.

Generally people who know nothing of this science think that it teaches merely the mechanical process of breathing in and out; but its province is much more extended, for it likewise shows how to control the Prâna, how to increase the vitality of the system by generating new nerve currents of a higher order, how to polarize the vibration of the cells, and how to awaken those powers which lie dormant on the sub-conscious plane as well as in the nerve centers of the spine. It also tells us that when the powers begin to manifest, we rise above the influences and changes to which ordinary mortals are subject. India is the only country where from ancient times this science of breathing has been carefully studied in all its aspects by the Yogis. Through centuries of investigation they discovered different methods of regulating the breath, following which marvellous results, both mental and physical, could be obtained. Out of these various discoveries grew up the science of breathing, which, besides the control of the breath, also explains what relation the process of respiration bears to Prâna, and how, by harmonizing the vibrations of nerve cells with the higher laws of life force, one gains mastery over Prâna. This control of Prâna brings complete subjugation of all the forces which govern the mind and body.

The aim of a Yogi is to establish absolute harmony between his vital actions and his mental functions, to transcend all laws, to rise above the influence of all environmental conditions, and to be the supreme ruler of the mind and of the entire system. According to the Yogi, this perfect self-mastery and consequent freedom do not come to one who has has not learned the secret of regulating the vital energy, and who has not acquired the power to direct it wherever it is needed. Before anyone can control this invisible vital force, he must know its principal seat in the body; he must learn where this unseen king of physical activities is enthroned, who are his attendants, and how he governs his kingdom.

A Yogi says that the king or Prâna resides with his attendants in the nerve centers of the spinal column. These centers are the main stations where this vital force is stored. There are many centers in the spinal cord out of which proceed the motor and sensory nerves which cover the whole body, including its organs. All sensations and motions of the limbs depend upon these nerve centers in the spinal column and the brain. There are two currents which flow in and out of the brain through the spinal column and nerves; they are called afferent and efferent currents—in Sanskrit, "Idâ" and "Pingalâ." They run through the anterior and posterior channels of the spinal cord, and these furnish the two paths over which the currents of Prâna travel. The nervous energy itself being scattered throughout the system, the only means of regulating it is by controlling the principal centers or stations in the spinal column. If, therefore, any one wishes to control the Prâna, he must first learn to govern the chief stations through which it works. After studying the relation of these different centers the Yogis found that there were six of primary importance. Those who wish to know their names can refer to the volume on "Râja Yoga" by the Swâmi Vivekânanda.

According to the science of breath, the King of these six leading nerve centers in the spinal cord is enthroned in the center opposite the thorax; it is the respiratory center and in Sanskrit bears the name "Anâhata." It moves the lungs, causes respiration, and gives activity to all the other centers, which are dependent on it. If the royal center is disturbed or vibrates abnormally, those which are subject to it, and through them the whole system will act in a corresponding manner; and the result will be disease, organic trouble, or continued ill-health. So long, however, as the royal center is in a normal condition, the movement of the lungs which causes inspiration and expiration will be regular. Therefore the Yogi who desires to subjugate the nerve centers first strives to gain control over the respiratory center. The science of breathing teaches that, by regulating the breath, the motion of the lungs and the functions of the whole nervous system can be regulated. It also says that, by controlling the nerve centers in the spinal column, mastery over the currents flowing throughout the system, and ultimately over the mind itself, with its various dormant powers, can be easily gained. If the mental powers that are now latent on the subconscious plane can be aroused, all the experiences of past incarnations, and the impressions gathered during previous lives, will come up on the conscious plane and we shall remember them all.

The Yogis say that the great majority of people breathe irregularly and that there are differences in the breathings of men and women. The causes of this irregular breathing are many—food, drink, fear, sickness, sorrow, nervous excitement, passion, anxiety. These do not affect the breath directly, but they do influence it indirectly by producing abnormal activity of Prâna, first in the nerve centers, then in the movement of the lungs, which expresses outwardly as irregular breathing. Hence irregularity of the breath is the external sign of abnormal action of the respiratory center in the spine.

A Yogi whose respiratory center functions regularly and is under perfect control is free from weakness, ill-health, and all disease. As, by controlling the activity of Prâna in the nerve centers, the movement of the lungs and the respiration are regulated, so, conversely, by regulating the breath, the lungs and nerve centers will be controlled, for they work simultaneously. Those who are suffering from ill-health should devote especial attention to the study of the science of breathing, as it is absolutely necessary to the building up of a healthy mind and a healthy body.

The chief aim of a Yogi is to observe his own nature closely and to learn clearly what forces are operating in his system, and what relation they bear to one another; for by gaining a complete knowledge of his own nature he will gain correct knowledge of the whole universe, since the laws that govern the human body are universal. All these laws are nothing but the modes in which Prâna operates in nature. Therefore a Yogi seeks first to understand the individual Prâna and the vital laws which govern his own system.

In India this fact was recognized and the science of breathing was carefully studied by the sages, who had no other ambition or purpose in life than to acquire knowledge for its own sake. They explained this science, practiced breathing exercises (noting the results), and instructed their pupils, but not to make a profession of it, or to earn money, or to gain fame in society. On the contrary, they refused to teach those who came to learn for professional ends; and it is because of this disinterestedness on their part that the knowledge of the Yogis is so pure and unadulterated by ambition or selfish motives. They also realized the dangers which might arise from ignorant practice of these exercises. Those who are studying under inexperienced teachers should be on their guard, for there is great risk in letting the nerve currents flow in a wrong direction. It may produce abnormal results and may even end in mental disorder. Right breathing, on the contrary, brings the greatest benefits to mankind when properly practiced; but if it is abused it must do a corresponding amount of harm, just as any medicine will when improperly applied. As by studying Materia Medica a man cannot cure himself without the aid of a trained physician, so the mere study of Yoga cannot bring about truly good results unless it is carried on under the guidance of an experienced Yogi. It should be remembered, furthermore, that in a written book everything is not given, that each constitution is different from every other, and that that which is helpful to one may not be so to another.

Anyone who practices faithfully, according to the instructions of an experienced living teacher, will surely gain highly beneficial results both in mind and body. He will learn how to manufacture vital force and to increase the vitality of his whole organism. He will be able to remove all impurities from his system and to overcome all abnormal and diseased conditions, that is, where decomposition and disorganization have not advanced too far. He will likewise no longer be a victim to cold, chills, Grip, fever, rheumatism, stiffness of the joints or muscles, paralysis, and other ills; for he knows how he can remove them by increasing the vibrations of Prâna and thus giving new life to the cells of the organs.

Every individual, whether old or young, man or woman, is bound to get some result if the breathing exercises be practiced faithfully for six months. By breathing exercises, however, is not meant here merely deep breathing, such as is taught by teachers of music, Delsarte, or physical culture. Deep breathing is very good for drawing a full supply or oxygen into the system, and undoubtedly has its value, especially for women who wear tight dresses. Many of the diseases from which they suffer are directly traceable to a lack of the adequate quantity of oxygen necessary for organic combustion and for the maintenance of the activity of the organs. The organs of many people in this country are undeveloped, or abnormally developed, because of the unnatural clothes worn; and for all such deep breathing will be exceedingly beneficial. But too much of it is injurious, as it inflates and strains the lungs, and, if continued, the increased development of the tissues will after a time decay and produce various troubles. Those who are taking lessons in deep breathing from inexperienced teachers should stop to consider this. By breathing exercises we mean that process by which control over the motion of the lungs and of the nerve centers, as also, in the end, over the Prâna or vital energy can be acquired.

A Yogi declares that the practice of

breathing will bring whatever result is desired, whether physical, psychical, or spiritual. He who has gained perfect control over his breath can suspend it for hours, and through this generate a power in the system which will levitate the body, even counteracting the tremendous force of gravitation. A Yogi conquers death by the control of Prâna. There are many Yogis in India who can tell the exact moment when they will leave their bodies. They say, "I am going to depart on such a day at such an hour," and at the appointed time consciously give up their bodies in the presence of many. There are some again who can prolong life indefinitely, and can subsist for long periods without taking any kind of solid or liquid food.

When so much can be accomplished through the control of the vital energy of

Prâna, it is not strange that these Masters say to the world:

"Oh, ye mortals, study the science of breathing; learn the secret of controlling Prâna or the vital energy; strive diligently to regulate the breath; for the control of Prâna will bring all happiness, earthly and spiritual, and through it will come perfect health, mastery of the body, and that Supreme Bliss which is eternal and everlasting.

Was Christ a Yogi?

Was Christ a Yogi?

In considering whether or not Christ was a Yogi we should first understand how spiritual and how divine one must be before he can be called a Yogi. A true Yogi must be pure, chaste, spotless, self-sacrificing, and the absolute master of himself. Humility, unostentatiousness, forgiveness, uprightness, and firmness of purpose must adorn his character. A true Yogi's mind should not be attached to sense-objects or sense-pleasures. He should be free from egotism, pride, vanity, and earthly ambition. Seeing the ephemeral nature of the phenomenal world, and reflecting upon the misery, suffering, sorrow, and disease with which our earthly existence is beset, he should renounce his attachment to external things, which produce but fleeting sensations of pleasure, and should overcome all that clinging to worldly life which is so strong in ordinary mortals.

A true Yogi does not feel happy when he is in the company of worldly-minded people who live on the sense plane like animals. He is not bound by family ties. He does not claim that this is his wife and these are his children; but, on the contrary, having realized that each individual soul, being a child of Immortal Bliss, belongs to the Divine Family, he severs all family relations and worldly connections and thus becomes absolutely free. A true Yogi must always preserve his equanimity in the face of the unpleasant as well as of the pleasant experiences of life; and rising above good and evil he should remain undisturbed by the success or failure, the victory or defeat, which may come to him as the result of the actions of his body and mind.

A true Yogi, again, must have unswerving devotion to the Supreme Spirit, the Almighty and Omniscient Soul of our souls; and realizing that his body and mind are the playground of the omnipotent Cosmic will, be should resign his individual will to the universal, and should be ever ready to work for others, to live for others, and to die for others. All his works, so long as he is in the society of people, should be a free offering to the world for the good of humanity; but at other times he should resort to secluded places and live alone, constantly applying his mind to the highest spiritual wisdom that can be obtained in the state of superconsciousness, through meditation on the oneness of the individual soul with God, the Universal Spirit.

A true Yogi must see the same Divinity dwelling in all living creatures. He should also love all human beings equally. He should have neither friend nor foe in the ordinary sense of those terms. A true Yogi is illumined by the light of Divine Wisdom, therefore nothing remains unknown to him. Time and space cannot limit the knowledge and wisdom of a true Yogi. Past and future events will appear to him like things happening before his eyes. For him the light of divine wisdom has dispelled the darkness of ignorance, which prevents one from realizing the true nature of the soul, and which makes one selfish, wicked, and sinful. All psychic and spiritual powers serve him as their real master. Whatever he says is sure to come to pass. He never utters a word in vain.

If he says to a distressed or suffering person, "Be thou whole," instantly that person will become whole.

The powers of a true Yogi are unlimited, there is nothing in the world that he cannot do. Indeed, he alone has free access to the storehouse of infinite powers; but he never draws therefrom any force merely to satisfy idle curiosity, or to gratify selfish motives, or to gain wealth and fame, or to get any return whatsoever. He does not seek worldly prosperity, and always remains unconcerned about the result of his works. Praise or censure does not disturb the peace of his mind. Angels or bright spirits and the spirits of ancestors rejoice in his company and adore him. A true Yogi is worshipped by all. Having neither home nor possessions of his own, he wanders from place to place, realizing that the canopy of heaven is the roof of his world-wide home. He is easily pleased by everybody irrespective of his caste, creed, or nationality, and with a loving heart he blesses those who rebuke or curse him. If his body be tortured or cut in pieces, he takes no revenge, but, on the contrary, prays for the welfare of his persecutor. Such is the character of a true Yogi.

From ancient times there have been many such true Yogis in India and other countries. The descriptions of their lives and deeds are furthermore as wonderful and as authentic as the life and acts of that illustrious Son of Man who preached in Galilee nearly two thousand years ago. The powers and works of this meek, gentle, and self-sacrificing Divine man, who is worshipped throughout Christendom as the ideal Incarnation of God and the Saviour of mankind, have proved that he was a perfect type of one who is called in

India a true Yogi. Jesus the Christ has been recognized by his disciples and followers not only as an exceptionally unique character but as the only-begotten Son of God; and it is quite natural for those who know nothing about the lives and deeds of similar ideal characters of great Yogis and Incarnations of God who have flourished at different times both before and after the Christian era, to believe that no one ever reached such spiritual heights or attained to such realization of oneness with the Heavenly Father as did Jesus of Nazareth.

The greater portion of the life of Jesus is absolutely unknown to us; and as He did not leave behind Him any systematic teaching regarding the method by which one may attain to that state of God-consciousness which He Himself reached, there is no way of finding out what He did or practiced during the eighteen years that elapsed before His appearance in public. It is, therefore, extremely difficult to form a clear conception of what path He adopted. But we can imagine that, being born with unusually developed spiritual inclinations, He must have devoted his life and time to such practices as led Him to the realization of absolute Truth and to the attainment of divine consciousness, which ultimately gave Him a place among the greatest spiritual leaders of the world as well as among the disinterested Saviours of mankind.

India is the only country where not only a complete system of practices is to be found, but also a perfect method, by following which well-qualified aspirants can attain to Christhood or to that spiritual unfoldment and divine enlightenment which made Jesus of Nazareth stand before the world as the ideal type of spiritual perfection. By studying the lives, the acts, and the most systematic and scientific teachings of the great Yogis of India, and by faithfully following their example and precepts, an earnest disciple can, through the Yoga practices given in the various branches of the Vedânta philosophy, hope some day to become as perfect as the Son of Man. This assurance must be a comfort and a consolation to the soul that is struggling for the attainment of spiritual perfection in this life. One peculiarity, however, of the teachings of the great Yogis of India is that the acquirement of spiritual perfection is the goal for all, and that each individual soul is bound, sooner or later, to be perfect even as Christ was perfect. They claim that spiritual truths and spiritual laws are as universal as the truths and laws of the material world, and that the realization of these truths cannot be confined to any particular time, place, or personality. Consequently by studying the Science of Yoga anyone can easily understand the higher laws and principles, an application of which will explain the mysteries connected with the lives and deeds of saints, sages, or Incarnations of God, like Krishna, Buddha, or Christ.

A genuine seeker after Truth does not limit his study to one particular example, but looks for similar events in the lives of all the great ones, and does not draw any conclusion until he has discovered the universal law which governs them all. For instance, Jesus the Christ said, "I and my Father are one." Did He alone say it, or did many others who lived before and after Him and who knew nothing of His sayings, utter similar expressions? Krishna declared, "I am the Lord of the universe." Buddha said, "I am the Absolute Truth." A Mahometan Sufi says, "I am He"; while every true Yogi declares, "I am Brahman." So long as we do not understand the principle that underlies such sayings, they seem mysterious to us and we cannot grasp their real meaning; but when we have realized the true nature of the individual soul, and its relation to the universal Spirit, or God, or Father in Heaven, or the Absolute Truth, we have learned the principle and there is no further mystery about it. We are then sure that whosoever reaches this state of spiritual oneness or God-consciousness will express the same thought in a similar manner. Therefore if we wish to understand the character and miraculous deeds of Jesus of Nazareth, the surest way open to us is the study of the Science of Yoga and the practice of its methods.

This Science of Yoga, as has already

been stated, explains all mysteries, reveals the causes of all miracles, and describes the laws which govern them. It helps us to unravel the secrets of nature and to discover the origin of such phenomena as are called miraculous. All miracles like "walking on the sea," "feeding a multitude with a small quantity of food," "raising the dead," which we read of in the life of Jesus, are described by the Yogis as manifestations of the powers that are acquired through long practice of Yoga. These powers are not supernatural; on the contrary, they are in nature, are governed by natural though higher laws, and are therefore universal. When these laws are understood, that which is ordinarily called miraculous by ignorant people, appears to be the natural result of finer forces working on a higher plane. There is no such thing as the absolutely supernatural. If a person's conception of nature be very limited, that which exists beyond that limit will seem to him supernatural, while to another, whose idea of nature is broader, the same thing will appear perfectly natural; therefore that miracle, or that particular act which is classed as a miracle by a Christian, can be explained by a Yogi as the result of higher or finer forces of nature. Why? Because his conception of nature is much wider than that of an ordinary man. We must not forget that nature is infinite, and that there are circles within circles, grades beyond grades, planes after planes, arranged in infinite succession; and the desire of a Yogi is to learn all the laws which govern these various planes, and to study every manifestation of force, whether fine or gross. His mind is not satisfied with the knowledge of one particular plane of existence; his aim is to comprehend the whole of nature.

Those who have read the gospel of Buddha, by Paul Carus, will remember that, five hundred years before the birth of Jesus the Christ, Shâriputra, Buddha's illustrious disciple, walked on the surface of the water across a mighty river named Shrâvasti. A similar account of crossing a wide river by walking on the water, we find in the life of Padmapâda, the disciple of Sankarâchârya, the best exponent of the Vedânta philosophy, who lived about 600 A.D. Krishna, the Hindu Christ, whose other name is Lord of the Yogis, raised the dead nearly fourteen hundred years before the advent of Christ. The transfiguration of Krishna is likewise most beautifully described in the tenth and eleventh chapters of the "Song Celestial," and, like Christ, he also fed a vast multitude of people with a small quantity of food. There are other instances of similar powers shown by great Yogis who came later; and these accounts are in every way as historical and as authentic as those of Jesus the Christ. Thus we see that all the miracles performed by Jesus are to be found as well in the lives of Hindu Yogis, who lived both before and after Him.

So long as an event is isolated it appears supernatural and miraculous; but if we see the same thing happening elsewhere under similar conditions, it assumes the aspect of a natural occurrence governed by natural law, and then comes a proper solution of the mystery as well as the rational explanation of that which was called a miracle. It is in this that the Science of Yoga renders especial service to the world, for more than any science it helps to reveal the secrets of nature and to explain the causes of all miraculous deeds.

A true Yogi goes to the source of all power and of all forces, studies the laws behind them, and learns the method of controlling them. He knows that the various forces of nature are but expressions of one universal, living, intelligent energy, which is called in Sanskrit "Prâna." He sees that all the forces of physical nature, like heat, gravitation, electricity, as also all mental forces such as mind, intellect, thought, are nothing but the manifestations of that one living self-existent force, "Prâna." This intelligent energy projects from its bosom innumerable suns, moons, stars, and planets into physical space. It has hurled this earth from the molten furnace of the sun, it has cooled it, bathed it in air and water, and clothed it with vegetable and animal life;

it wings the atmosphere with clouds and spans the planes with rivers, it takes a fine minute substance and transforms it into something huge and gross; it moves the body, gives life and motion to every atom and molecule, and at the same time manifests itself as thought and intellect.

Why should it be impossible for one who has realized his oneness with this fountainhead of all power, who has learned the method of controlling all phenomena by comprehending the laws which govern them, and who has become the master of the world as was Jesus the Christ, to perform simple phenomena like walking on the sea, turning water into wine, or raising the dead? According to a true Yogi these acts of Jesus the Christ were only a few expressions of the Yoga powers which have been exercised over and over again by the Yogis in India. Thus we understand that

Christ was one of these great Yogis born in a Semitic family.

Jesus was a great Yogi because He realized the transitory and ephemeral nature of the phenomenal world, and, discriminating the real from the unreal, renounced all desire for worldly pleasures and bodily comforts. Like a great Yogi He lived a life of seclusion, cutting off all connections with earthly friends and relatives, and having neither home nor possessions of His own.

Jesus the Christ was a great Karma Yogi, because He never worked for results; He had neither desire for name nor ambition for fame or for earthly prosperity. His works were a free offering to the world. He labored for others, devoted His whole life to help others, and in the end died for others. Being unattached to the fruits of His actions, He worked incessantly for the good of His fellow-men, directing them to the path of righteousness and spiritual realization through unselfish works. He understood the law of action and reaction, which is the fundamental principle of Karma Yoga, and it was for this reason that He declared, "Whatsoever a man soweth, that shall he also reap."

Jesus of Nazareth proved Himself to be a great Bhakti Yogi, a true lover of God, by His unswerving devotion and His wholehearted love for the Heavenly Father. His unceasing prayers, incessant supplications, constant meditation, and unflinching self-resignation to the will of the Almighty made Him shine like a glorious morning-star in the horizon of love and devotion of a true Bhakti Yogi. Christ showed wonderful self-control and mastery over His mind throughout the trials and sufferings which were forced upon Him. His sorrow, agony, and self-surrender at the time of His death as well as before His crucifixion, are conclusive proofs that He was a human being with those divine qualities which adorn the soul of a true Bhakti Yogi. It is true that His soul labored for a while under the heavy burden of His trials and sufferings; it is also true that He felt that His pain was becoming wellnigh unbearable when He cried aloud three times, praying to the Lord, "O my Father, if it be possible, let this cup pass from me." But He found neither peace nor consolation until He could absolutely resign His will to that of the Father and could say from the bottom of His heart, "Thy will be done." Complete self-surrender and absolute self-resignation are the principal virtues of Bhakti Yoga, and as Christ possessed these to perfection up to the last moment of His life, He was a true Bhakti Yogi.

Like the great Râja Yogis in India, Jesus knew the secret of separating His soul from His physical shell, and He showed this at the time of His death, while His body was suffering from extreme pain, by saying, "Father, forgive them, for they know not what they do." It is quite an unusual event to see one imploring forgiveness for his persecutors while dying on the cross, but from a Yogi's point of view it is both possible and natural. Râmakrishna, the greatest Yogi of the nineteenth century, whose life and sayings have been written by Max Müller, was once asked, "How could Jesus pray for His persecutors when He was in agony on the cross?" Râmakrishna answered by an illustration: "When the shell of an ordinary green cocoanut is pierced through, the nail enters the kernel of the nut too. But in the case of the dry nut the kernel becomes separate from the shell, and so when the shell is pierced, the kernel is not touched. Jesus was like the dry nut, i.e., His inner soul was separate from His physical shell, and consequently the sufferings of the body did not affect him." * Therefore He could pray for the forgiveness of His persecutors even when His body was suffering; and all true Yogis are able to do the same. There have been many instances of Yogis whose bodies have been cut into pieces, but their souls never for a moment lost that peace and equanimity which enabled Jesus to forgive and bless His persecutors. By this Christ proved that, like other Yogis, His soul was completely emancipated from the bondage

* See "The Life and Sayings of Râmakrishna," by Prof. F. Max Müller. Published by Charles Scribners' Sons, New York. P. 111.

of the body and of the feelings. Therefore Christ was a Yogi.

Through the path of devotion and love Jesus attained to the realization of the oneness of the individual soul with the Father or the Universal Spirit, which is the ideal of a Jnâna Yogi as well as the ultimate goal of all religions. A Jnâna Yogi says: "I am He"; "I am Brahman"; "I am the Absolute Truth"; "I am one with the Supreme Deity." By good works, by devotion, love, concentration, contemplation, long fasting, and prayer, Jesus the Christ realized that His soul was one with God, therefore He may be said to have attained the ideal of Jnâna Yoga.

Like Krishna, Buddha, and all other great Yogis of India, Jesus healed the sick, opened the eyes of the blind, made the lame walk, and read the secret thoughts of His disciples. He knew exactly what Judas and Peter were going to do; but there was nothing supernatural in any of His actions, there was nothing that cannot be done again over and over by a true Yogi, and there was nothing in His life that cannot be explained rationally by the Science of Yoga and the Philosophy of Vedânta. Without the help of this science and this philosophy Jesus the Christ cannot be fully understood and appreciated. By studying His character, on the other hand, in the light of the Vedânta Philosophy we shall be able not only to understand Him better, but to have a larger appreciation of His true glory.

Material science now scoffs at His miracles, but they are corroborated by the Science of Yoga and confirmed by the deeds of the great Yogis of India. No devout Christian need for a moment fear that physical science can ever undermine the work of Jesus so long as the Science of Yoga is there to sustain all that He did. Let him study the character of Jesus through the Philosophy of Vedânta and I am sure that he will understand Him better and be a truer Christian, a more genuine disciple of the Son of Man than ever before. Let him follow the teachings of Yoga and he will some day become perfect like Christ.

It is through the teachings of Vedânta that the Hindus have learned how to glorify the character of Jesus; so also it is through Vedânta that a Christian will learn to adore the great Yogis like Krishna, Buddha, Râmakrishna, and others. It is through Vedânta that a Christian will be able to see how Divinity dwells in all animate and inanimate objects, and thus comprehending the true relation of the individual soul to the Supreme Spirit, will be enabled to say with the great Yogi Jesus the Christ, "I and my Father are one," and reach salvation in this life.